The Math We Need to "Know" and "Do"

CORWIN
PRESS

The Corwin Press logo—a raven striding across an open book—represents the happy union of courage and learning. We are a professional-level publisher of books and journals for K–12 educators, and we are committed to creating and providing resources that embody these qualities. Corwin's motto is "Success for All Learners."

Pearl Gold Solomon

The Math We Need to "Know" and "Do"

Content Standards for Elementary and Middle Grades

CORWIN PRESS, INC.
A Sage Publications Company
Thousand Oaks, California

For information:

Corwin Press, Inc.
A Sage Publications Company
2455 Teller Road
Thousand Oaks, California 91320
E-mail: order@corwinpress.com

Sage Publications Ltd.
6 Bonhill Street
London EC2A 4PU
United Kingdom

Sage Publications India Pvt. Ltd.
M-32 Market
Greater Kailash I
New Delhi 110 048 India

Printed in the United States of America

Library of Congress Cataloging-in-Publication Data

Solomon, Pearl G. (Pearl Gold), 1929–
    The math we need to "know" and "do": Content standards for elementary
and middle grades / by Pearl Gold Solomon.
        p.   cm.
    Includes bibliographical references.
    ISBN 0-7619-7577-2 (pbk.: acid-free paper)
    1. Mathematics—Study and teaching (Elementary)—United States
    2. Mathematics—Study and teaching (Middle school)—United States
    I. Title.
    QA135.5 .S5715 2000
    372.7—dc21   00-009203

This book is printed on acid-free paper.

01   02   03   04   05   06   10   9   8   7   6   5   4   3   2   1

Corwin Editorial Assistant:	Catherine Kantor
Production Editor:	Denise Santoyo
Editorial Assistant:	Cindy Bear
Typesetter/Designer:	Marion Warren
Cover Designer:	Michelle Lee

CONTENTS

GUIDE TO FIGURES IN CHAPTER 3

What This Book Is About

Never has there been such public awareness of the problems of our educational systems—and never so much criticism. Not the least of that criticism has been directed at the performance of our students in mathematics, especially when it is compared to that of students from other countries on international tests such as the Third International Mathematics and Science Study (TIMSS) (Schmidt, McNight, & Raizen, 1996). Although there are a number of possible reasons for this poor performance, much of the blame has fallen on U.S. schools and teachers. This may be unfair, but there is some recent evidence that our curriculum is a culprit. It covers too many topics repetitively and lacks intensity and focus. Most of what is taught in schools today is governed by published texts and workbooks, and many of our new generation of teachers are the products of that same kind of

math instruction. Frequently, our students learn how to do the procedures in the books without constructing mathematical concepts that may be generalized to novel, real-life problems.

There is much that is worthwhile in today's textbooks for young learners; they provide drill and practice for operations and some good and varied application activities. First-generation computer software has enhanced these by making the same activities more interesting and diverse, and by providing control and immediate feedback to the student. New-generation technology, such as graphing calculators and software that allows for exploration and spatial problem solving, as well as access to data sets on the Internet, is even more hopeful, if used properly. The deficiency lies in the fact that this technology does not clearly delineate for teachers or students what exactly one needs to know in order to be an effective quantitative problem solver: the mathematical concepts. Nor does it help teachers understand and build upon what research has taught us about how learning happens. Pedagogical texts for teachers do this, but often they, too, neglect the concepts.

Strangely, very old mathematics textbooks stated very clearly and simply what the necessary concepts were. *New Practical Arithmetic,* written by Benjamin Greenleaf (1872), brings the learner from the very elementary notations of single-digit numbers all the way to cube roots and the applications of stocks, bonds, taxes, principal, and interest within 322 small (4- by 6-inch) pages. On these pocket-size pages are 465 paragraph sections that include precise definitions and succinct statements of the concepts, as well as limited exercises. What Greenleaf did establish, for his time, was a clear mathematical knowledge base.

Although the world has gained much new knowledge since 1872, and topics such as probability, statistics, and mathematical modeling have to be added to help prepare our students for the modern world, the basic known content or knowledge base of elementary mathematics is not that different. Nevertheless, our pedagogical knowledge base, especially our knowledge about how children learn, is much expanded. We use many new and better approaches to learning and teaching. Preoccupation with this new pedagogical knowledge has perhaps distracted us from the mathematics knowledge itself.

This book focuses primarily on the mathematics content, but restates it in the current context of expanded pedagogical knowledge. It covers content that is traditionally introduced through the sixth grade and carries the development of it into the seventh and eighth grades. The book introduces some newly important concepts as well, but other topics traditionally included for the first time at the seventh-grade level and above are not included.

It is designed as a resource for teachers to use as they

▷ Plan curriculum for a school, particular grade level, or specific lesson

▷ Assess their students' knowledge, both formally and informally

▷ Respond to individual conceptual or procedural problems among their students

▷ Review their own mathematical concepts

Like Greenleaf, we have tried to be parsimonious with words. For in-depth discussions of the background research, readers can refer to the literature cited in our references. This is also not a mathematics textbook, although it will provide some illustrative activities for students. Instead, it will compensate for the missing components of recent texts— statements of the specific concepts and procedures embedded in mathematical knowledge. These are phrased, succinctly and precisely, in the new terminology of *content standards* and their articulated measures, *performance standards.*

The standards statements in this book are different from most curriculum guides in their greater specificity. They tell us more exactly what students need to know and to be able to do in order to solve the problems in the texts and on the new state assessments. They tell us some of what the students need to know in order to have lifelong comfort and ease with new mathematical problems and to compete with others in a technological future. They will help teachers analyze whether their students have achieved the specifics of that knowledge, and guide them in the correction of unsound or incomplete constructions of knowledge.

This book is a resource meant to be used by teachers in conjunction with other materials: texts, workbooks, manipulatives, and technology. It can also serve as an adjunct textbook for teachers-in-training—one that focuses more intensely on the content as it applies rather than generalizes the pedagogy. To accomplish our purpose of clarity in the presentation of the concepts, the content standards and their matching performance standards are presented in table form as Chapter 2. The illustrative enactment or assessment activities are articulated with matching numbers, but presented separately, in Chapter 3.

There are clear purposes for this separation. Chapter 2 can be used to plan a school's curriculum from a multigrade or single-grade perspective. Teachers can use it as a daily assessment check and lesson-planning guide, and with an easy reference look back at the grounding concepts from previous grades. If further clarification is needed, or if the teacher needs suggestions for how to scaffold the concept with dialogue and problems to solve, there is a simple cross-check to the more comprehensive Chapter 3. However, no single or even set of activities is guaranteed to ensure the new knowledge for all students. Just doing a prescribed activity is not enough; the embedded concept has to be constructed and applied by the student and assessed by the teacher.

Although there are suggestions offered for the vocabulary and substance of the teacher-directed dialogues and peer interactive discourses that can help students construct new knowledge, this is far from a script. It is different from many curriculum guides produced by teachers in that it shows the sequential and specific development of concepts over the grades, rather than at a specific grade. The reason for this is so that teachers may check for prior knowledge and know where a particular concept may lead. It is hoped that this will make their curriculum more responsive to the individual differences among their students.

The concepts or content standards included are a composite from many sources. Many were identified over time by careful personal and shared collegial observation of students' thinking: from prekindergarten through graduate classes in math teaching methods. They reflect mathematics educators' most current research on how children learn mathematics, as reported in the literature, but also pull from resources as disparate and remote as Piaget, Greenleaf, and a comprehensive curriculum guide published by the Baltimore schools in 1952 (Baltimore Public Schools, 1952; Greenleaf, 1872; Piaget, 1926, 1977). They are functionally based on the ideas and organization of the new standards for mathematics developed by the National Council of Teachers of Mathematics (NCTM) and other state and local agencies (National Council of Teachers of Mathematics, 2000). These are more comprehensive in terms of the pedagogy and its rationale and therefore should be consulted in tandem with this book.

The NCTM standards are, however, less specific and organized about the content knowledge, particularly the underlying concepts and definitions. This leaves much for the teacher to provide. For example, the standards statements are often framed in terms of understanding, such as "Students will understand the relationship between multiplication and division." Chapter 2, and certainly Chapter 3, are more explicit about what students need to understand. Concept statements and scaffolds for building understanding would include ideas such as, "In multiplication, we know the size of each group and the number of the groups we add repeatedly, but not the size of the whole. We multiply to find the whole.

In division, we know the whole and either the number of groups or the size of the group, but not both. We divide to find the size of each group or the number of groups."

This book will fill in some of the gaps, but certainly not every possible construction of knowledge. Others may be identified or newly constructed by teachers as they begin to teach in a different way—with a clearly identified concept or construct in mind. If they provide opportunities for their students to reason and solve problems creatively, new concepts for both teacher and student may be intersubjectively constructed.

The book is presented in three chapters, which should be considered in sequence. Chapter 1 provides a rationale for the suggested learning approach and explains the organization and sequence of the following chapters. Chapter 2 provides the actual content standards in numbered table form, showing median grade-level expectations for content and performance standards, as well as suggestions for mathematics language vocabulary and usage. The content standards are organized to agree with the organization of the NCTM standards, with some exceptions that are explained in Chapter 1. Chapter 3 provides articulated, illustrative activities and problems that can be used with students, for either concept development or assessment purposes. It also contains suggestions for using materials other than text: manipulatives, calculators, educational software and graphics programs (commercial and shareware), and Web sites.

Acknowledgments

I would like to thank several people for their assistance in creating this book. My students, Ann Mohr and Charlene Knel, practicing math teachers, and Kees DeGroot, Professor of Math Education at SUNY New Paltz, read the manuscript with keen and knowing eyes, and my colleague, Sr. Teresa O'Connor, offered support and helpful comments. My grandsons, Joseph and Edward Burke, kept me well informed of the culture of elementary and middle-grade students, inspired me, tried the problems, and offered suggestions. Alice Foster, my acquiring editor at Corwin Press, was, as usual, a patient and strong motivator, who kept me moving on this project. My husband, Mel, always supportive, kept my confidence and drive to complete a challenging task at an optimum.

ABOUT THE AUTHOR

Pearl Gold Solomon is Professor of Education at St. Thomas Aquinas College, where she teaches graduate and undergraduate courses, and Director of the Marie Curie Math and Science Center, which provides math, science, and technology enrichment experiences for 5th- to 12th-grade students, and professional development for inservice teachers. She earned her EdD from Teachers College, Columbia University. Her 41 years of experience in public education, grades K-12, include being an elementary and high school teacher, middle school principal, and a director of curriculum. She is the author of *No Small Feat* (1995), and *The Curriculum Bridge* (1998), which was recently selected for inclusion in the American Library Association's list of Outstanding Academic Titles for 1999. In addition to these, Solomon has written, delivered, and published a number of papers describing her research. She has been the recipient of grants from the New York State Education Department and the National Science Foundation, and served as a consultant to the United States Office of Education as well as to many school districts, including those in the cities of New York and Chicago. She has two daughters, is actively involved with two spirited grandsons, and in February 2000 celebrated 50 years of marriage to her husband Milton.

CHAPTER 1

Designing a Standards-Based Math Curriculum

Knowledge

Education is preparation for life. Derived from the Latin, it also means *to lead forth*—perhaps to knowledge. But what is the knowledge to which we educators must lead our students? Knowledge is defined as an acquaintance with a fact, a perception, an idea. A suggested classification of knowledge divides it into procedural and conceptual components. The two categories are distinguishable and yet intersecting. They are not hierarchical; one does not necessarily come before the other. They differ in that procedural knowledge is more rigid and limited in its adaptability, but highly efficient, especially when it is applied with meaning. Conceptual knowledge is more flexible—it reorganizes and stretches itself as it tries to connect new perceptions and previous generalizations. Conceptual knowledge may then re-form itself as a new generalization. Reasoning requires conceptual knowledge (for an in-depth

discussion of conceptual and procedural knowledge, see Hiebert and Lefevre, 1986).

A chef following an often-used recipe is efficiently carrying out his procedural knowledge. He knows that it must be done in a certain order and with specific ingredients and quantities. Suppose one of his ingredients is unavailable. He has a problem. When he tries to innovate with a substitute ingredient, he calls upon his conceptual knowledge; reorganizes it; connects it to other concepts and perhaps to a new generalization; and then, with practice, connects it to a new procedure. The best procedures are those built with conceptual knowledge, those learned with meaning. Conceptual knowledge may, however, also come from procedural knowledge. An infant puts blocks one on top of the other, perhaps in a self-initiated procedure or perhaps copying an adult. Eventually, a concept is formed: The larger blocks need to be at the bottom. *The conceptual and procedural knowledge components that we expect our students to have, and to which we must lead them, form our content standards.* Our expectations are based on our own knowledge, our experience, and our predictions about what our students will need. Content standards describe what we value and want our students to know or be able to do.

The reason for the discussion above is that in the past, mathematics has often been taught as a set of specific procedures, sometimes disconnected from the real problems that will confront us in life. Doing mathematics requires a set of concepts and procedures that develops over time. Experiences with objects and verbalization—both monologic and interactive—help that development. The concepts enlarge our capability to solve problems; the procedures make us more efficient. An understanding of this dual nature of knowledge also provides a rationale for the organization of a standards-based curriculum.

Organization and Design of Curricula

Although concepts and procedures develop individually for each student over time, it is useful for the teacher to know what the necessary ones are—the ones that can help the student do mathematics and solve mathematical problems. The common procedures we use and some of the concepts we share are in what has been called "the consensual domain" (Cobb, 1990). This shared knowledge is the content of our curriculum. The framework for curriculum content includes normed expectations for achievement, or *standards*. The multiplication facts are shared knowledge in the consensual domain. That we expect third and fourth graders to know their multiplication facts is a normed expectation or standard

based on history, teachers' experience, and the average achievements of children in these grades. *Content standards* organize and describe the curriculum. They serve as guides for instruction that are planned to help students achieve the knowledge of the consensual domain. They tell us what students should know or be able to do. In addition, in order to measure the achievement of the content standards, we can turn the content standards into matching *performance standards,* or, indicators that give us measurement guidelines. They tell us "How good is good enough?" When constructed, the performance standards should be reflections of the content standards they measure. An analogy that might help is to compare them to the two sides of your hand. The back of your hand defines its form and its potential, but the palm is the implement and measure of what your hand does. Performance standards frame the assessments we need to make to help guide our instruction and students, and provide accountability to our public.

Standards can be very general statements of expectations at a terminal or commencement point, or more specific and assigned to a particular stage in development or grade level. The upside-down tree in Figure 1.1 illustrates a design process for standards-based curricula (Solomon, 1998). Like the trunk of a tree, general standards lead to a widely reaching set of more specific branches, twigs, and leaves. The curriculum is *designed down* from more general *commencement* levels to the more specific *benchmarks,* and then to the even more specific levels of the course, grade, and unit. But it must work both ways. Just as the leaves of a tree must manufacture food and nurture the trunk, the more specific designed-down content standards of every lesson must feed the general ones—they make the general ones happen. Curriculum is *delivered up*—up toward the general or commencement

Figure 1.1. Curriculum Planning

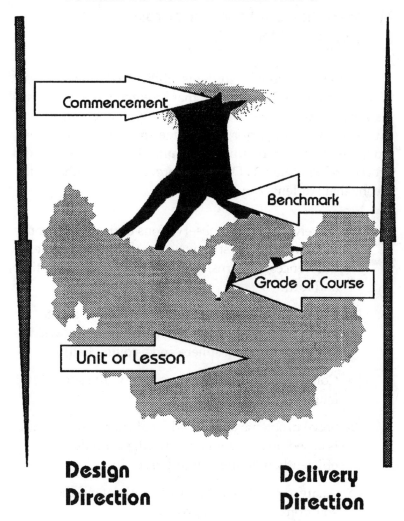

CURRICULUM PLANNING

Commencement

Benchmark

Grade or Course

Unit or Lesson

Design Direction

Delivery Direction

standards. None of this works if the connections of internal flow are impeded. The junctures where twigs meet branches and branches meet trunks are particularly important. The outcome of each lesson of the leaves is fed through a twig to the branch that is the unit and then into a larger one that is the grade level. Several grade levels may feed into a larger branch at a benchmark juncture, and this, in turn, finally meets the main trunk. The tree is shown upside down because the design is the beginning, and we think of the processes as "design down" and "deliver up." At the same time, there must be horizontal articulation. As the leaves turn toward the sun, the carbon dioxide must enter them. There must be a balance between the concepts and the procedures.

The preplanned design is only the first step. The settings and activities of well-planned classroom instruction must have a reasonable probability of helping *all* students to be successful in these measures. They should encompass a wider scope of the variables of the classroom experience: the teacher's knowledge and carefully reviewed previous experience, the discourse, the materials, the allocation of time and space, and the cultural and social contexts of peers and adults.

The Mathematics Content Standards: Key Ideas[1]

What kind of mathematical knowledge do we expect of all students as they enter our new technological world of the third millennium? What are the steps for getting them there? Consider the upside-down tree for mathematics curricula.

Beginning at the trunk, at the commencement level, we should expect that *all* students can do the processes of mathematics.

Nevertheless, the processes of mathematics are not performed in a vacuum. They depend upon and produce a content set of conceptual and procedural knowledge about mathematics. However, before we address the specifics of the processes and content knowledge standards, there are some *key ideas* that should be considered.

▷ In its traditional sense, mathematical *reasoning* includes quantitative, qualitative, and spatial concepts, but it also has embedded *verbal constructs and a special language.* These constructs may affect the power of the reasoning.

▷ The special language of mathematical *communication* involves a system of *numbers and other symbols.* The symbols represent values and orders, or something that changes the value. Not only do we need to use this language to communicate with others, but the symbols and words may also be necessary for our own internal concept formation. There is also a special language for sharing proof.

▷ A logical search for truth or *proof* requires reasoning and is a special power of mathematics. Proof to oneself also strengthens the constructions of knowledge.

▷ As we observe, reason, connect, and communicate, we can develop and use an intuitive *number and spatial sense* that allows us to estimate values, judge relative size, visualize hidden parts of forms, decide on appropriate strategies for problem solving, predict the result of operations and transformations, and evaluate the reasonableness of our problem solutions.

Mathematics Content Standards: Processes and Dispositions

Our expectations of students' ability to do the processes of mathematics reflect the way that research has shown us all learning happens; like all learning, doing mathematics involves connecting prior knowledge and new perceptions. Doing mathematics requires and builds both conceptual and procedural knowledge. Doing the processes of mathematics means that students can

▷ Perceive and make observations of the world from a mathematical perspective, sensitive to similarities, differences, patterns, and change in size, value, time, and form

▷ Connect these observations to each other and to other concurrent observations and prior knowledge (e.g., the form of a sphere and a rolling ball)

▷ Communicate what they perceive in the special language of mathematics

▷ Solve problems using mathematical reasoning, which is based on conceptual knowledge, and do this efficiently with meaningful procedures

▷ Analyze problems and justify and defend their solutions with logical proofs

Conceptual knowledge can also be knowledge about oneself; it can be an attitude or a value. Attitudes and values control the learning process. Doing mathematics also requires that students

▷ Have confidence in their ability to do mathematics

▷ Appreciate the beauty and power of mathematics

Mathematics Content Standards: The Knowledge Content Set

For the purpose of description, we can organize the knowledge content set into seven major branches. It is important to realize, however, that these branches are overlapping, both in their interdependence and in their function as we enact mathematical processes. For example, our operations are dependent on our number system, and our number system determines the form of our operations. We need knowledge of our number system, measurement, and data representation as we communicate to others what we have perceived. The content standards described in Chapter 2 include designed-down concepts and procedures from the following commencement-level branches:

▷ *Number system:* The language of our common number system (which is based on our genetically and experientially determined sense of space and quantity and the number of finger or toe digits) allows us to perceive and communicate quantities in words and symbols. By making the left-to-right position of the symbols have different values, we are able to express all quantities with only 10 symbols,

including the placeholder zero. There are other number systems.

▷ *Operations on numbers:* We can perform operations on numbers. Operations are systems that help us solve problems that involve change or comparisons. They allow us to determine values not directly counted or measured. Reasoning with our conceptual knowledge and using our number sense can help us predict the result of operations. The language of real-world problems needs to be translated into the language of mathematics so that we can solve the problems efficiently by performing operations.

▷ *Geometric forms and properties:* Defined, two-dimensional surface areas and three-dimensional objects that take up space have different geometric forms and properties. Knowledge of the dimensions and properties of these forms, and the relationships among them, helps us solve problems and make use of the systematic relationship between the types of forms and their practical functions (e.g., the rolling sphere, the Roman arch, the sturdy triangle).

▷ *Measurement and data collection:* We use our number system to measure the dimensions and characteristics of objects and areas as they exist or change in time and space. We also measure time itself and other values and phenomena, such as money, light, wind, energy, votes, and the popularity of TV shows. Collections of measurements are called *data*.

▷ *Patterns and mathematical functions—Algebra:* Within the systems of numbers, forms, and data, there are recognizable patterns. Patterns help us reason, organize, and automatize concepts into more efficient procedures. We can use *symbols* to show these patterns. The symbols can represent either variable or constant values. When patterns are systems that describe relationships between variable values, they are called *mathematical functions* (as distinguished from practical functions). Conceptual and procedural knowledge of functions is very useful in complex problem solving and prediction.

▷ *Models and multiple representations:* Models and multiple representations of forms and number systems help us visualize, communicate mathematical ideas, and organize data, but they also help us construct concepts and are useful for simple and complex procedures and problem solutions.

▷ *Probability:* Some events are clearly predictable, but others are uncertain. Probability systems help us deal with uncertainty by giving us a way to have reasonable expectations about the possibility of the occurrence of an event.

The Presentation of Designed-Down Standards in Chapter 2

Chapter 2 takes the major branches or benchmarks of the mathematical *content standards* that are listed in the previous section and designs them down to minor branches and some very specific things that students should know. The designed-down content standards answer questions such as, What is it in the division operations branch that you need to know before you can solve problems that require the

Figure 1.2.

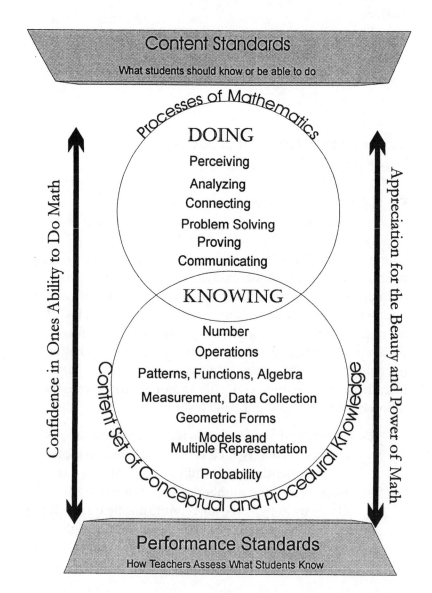

operation? What do you look for when you *analyze* the problems? What facts and patterns should you quickly recall to make solutions more obvious? How do you do the procedures of the division algorithm? Why do they make sense? How can you divide by a decimal? How is division connected to fractions? How can you *prove* the relationship between division and multiplication?

The designed-down *performance standards* tell the teacher what the students must be able to do to prove that they know the matching content standards. Can students *communicate* in their *analysis* with words and/or appropriate representations that they are able to distinguish whether a particular problem requires them to divide a whole group into a given number of parts and find out how large each part is, or whether it asks them how many parts of a given size will be in the whole?

The presentation of very specific designed-down content and performance standards in Chapters 2 and 3 incorporates several critical premises about what students need, how learning happens, and how teachers use the curriculum. The organization of these chapters respond to these premises in the specific manner as described below.

▷ *Premise 1: Inclusivity* Although Chapters 2 and 3 represent most of the topics traditionally introduced through grade 6, they do not pretend to be all-inclusive, neither of the topics nor of the underlying concepts that form the content and performance standards. Two hundred concept sections may be just a starting place. Teachers and their students may discover additional ones and make some corrections. What is important is to recognize and communicate these concepts to oneself and to others.

▷ *Premise 2: Timing* For some concepts, and for some students, learning happens all at once. For many others, it is an iterative process that takes place over time as students develop meaning in a very individualized way. Sometimes, this meaning has flaws or is incorrect, and is corrected by new perceptions. Therefore, the grade-level expectations in Chapter 2 are presented in three phases: exploration, concept mastery, and procedural or algorithmic mastery. In some cases, this sequence may happen within one grade—even within one lesson; in others, the span may be longer than three grades. The expectations listed are suggested medians based on observations of students and references to varied texts and assessments. Teachers should adjust these on a local basis. The idea behind the three phases is that as students engage in the mathematical processes, they begin with explorations: perceiving, observing, trying to find solutions. At first, they may find solutions without crystallizing a concept that is permanently implanted as a schema in memory. They may need help from teachers and/or peers in the form of interactive dialogue to do this.

▷ *Premise 3: Algorithms* Once the concept is formed, further experience may automate its retrieval from memory, and learners can incorporate it into strategies or procedures that can be employed efficiently. The common algorithms are an example of procedural strategies. The algorithms were invented over time as efficient procedures for solving common mathematics problems. Students should be able to use the algorithms in the consensual domain but are encouraged to invent and prove their own strategies as well. A good rule of thumb for the use of traditional algorithms by students is to evaluate the potential usefulness of the algorithm—as a tool for solving real problems in the current technological world; as a written record that might help organize concepts; and as a procedure, learned in its application to simple, easily understood problems, that can then be extrapolated to more complex applications. In the past, much time has been spent by students in the process of developing skill, speed, and accuracy in using these algorithms—perhaps detracting from a focus on the more powerful ideas of mathematics and distracting students from interpretations of problems that would allow for quick mental solutions. These algorithms were most often learned without attention to understanding how and why they worked. Analysis of problems hinged on key words that told you which algorithm to use; the selected procedure was applied without conceptual understanding or recognition that sometimes the problem could be easily solved mentally.

Students should be encouraged to use their concept-based number or spatial sense to interpret a problem and estimate its answer before applying a procedure. They may, however, need the teacher's help and some practice to reach the third procedural mastery phase. In some cases, when the child's struggle with the construction of a concept is discouraging, it may even be necessary to move over the concept to a rotely learned procedure. But attempts to recursively revive the concept should continue. In general, moving to a procedure first should be avoided because there is some evidence that learning a procedure rotely—without the underlying concepts—may encumber concept development and handicap further development of mathematical processes.

▷ *Premise 4: Automaticity* In order to be able to estimate and use reasoning to solve problems, students need a repertoire of easily retrieved bits of conceptual and procedural knowledge. That repertoire includes related addition and subtraction facts for combinations up to 20 and multiplication and division tables to 12, as well as the standard unit equivalents for measurement. We use the term *automaticity* as an outcome to differentiate from the traditional term, *memorized,* in order to emphasize that the process of imprinting the facts should be a meaningful one, using reasoning and pattern recognition. Automaticity implies fast retrieval from memory, but, strengthened by the conceptual knowledge of patterns, it also allows for fast reconstruction should a fact be temporarily lost.

▷ *Premise 5: Language* Although I have tried to use clear and simplified language, the words of the content standards are adult terms that express the consensual domain. It is not necessary for children to use the exact words as long as the teacher is convinced that the meaning has been constructed correctly. In some cases, the children will be able to demonstrate the concept only by doing things with objects or giving examples, but verbalization of the concept in different ways should be encouraged and listened to. In order to verbalize, children need a shared language. The special language of mathematics, in both symbolic and word form, should be attended to specifically.

▷ *Premise 6: Embedded Assessment* The performance standards can be used for formal assessments, but they are also designed to be embedded in the everyday activities, in the dialogues, and in the questions and cues that teachers toss to students to help them construct new knowledge or correct preexisting concepts.

▷ *Premise 7: Embedded Processes* As discussed previously, the process standards and content branches are constantly overlapping. In response to this integrated nature of knowledge, there are no separate sections for the processes. Instead, they are embedded in the content and performance standards. There is some organization of the content branches based on developmental expectations and traditional presentations, but even these are addressed as overlapping segments.

▷ *Premise 8: Representative Materials* Concrete materials, including real and representative manipulatives, increase the possibilities of mathematical perceptions and provide useful, often indispensable, problem-solving strategies as they lead to concept formation. Manipulatives respond to individual differences in learning styles and forms of intelligence, increasing the feelings of self-efficacy for those who are more kinesthetic or tactile in their learning approach. They are particularly helpful at the early levels, when children are still at a concrete operational stage, and sometimes even necessary for adults whose concepts need to be redeveloped. However, we need to remember that representative manipulatives are, in essence, analogies for the real thing, and conscious connections have to be made. Further transitions have to be constructed carefully as children move from the concrete materials to the symbolic forms. The words of everyday language count as well. There needs to be interactive dialogue connecting the words that explain the concept, the manipulatives, and the written symbols of the language of mathematics.

Learners vary in their need for manipulatives and sometimes reject them once the concept or efficient procedure has been developed. They can become cumbersome when dealing with large numbers, and teachers need to use their best judgment about whether they are of value once the underlying concept is developed. A good rule of thumb is to use the materials to introduce concepts and abandon them for most students when the students have made a conceptual shift to the symbolic form or operation. For some students, teachers will have to return to the concrete materials in remedial or small group sessions.

▷ *Premise 9: Problem-Solving Strategies* There are other problem-solving strategies that teachers may help students develop. In general, connections to real-life situations work as they retrieve prior knowledge and provide motivation. Other strategies include

▶ Acting out the problem with physical movements (e.g., touching each item for one-to-one correspondence)

▶ Making a picture or concept map, or organizing given data on a table

▶ Purposeful analysis of problems based on their underlying specific concepts. This may also be considered a general strategy, but one that is dependent on the concepts themselves. We will make specific suggestions for these concept-based strategies in Chapter 3, but they are also embedded in the performance standards.

▷ *Premise 10: Technology* Calculators and computers are not substitutes for the conceptual and procedural knowledge needed for automaticity in retrieval of basic facts, number and spatial sense, and process skills, nor should they take away from the teacher-managed and peer-interactive discourse of doing mathematics. But they can help the students build knowledge. They are, in a way, our modern algorithms—short-cut procedures for complex computations—just as the wristwatch is a technological substitute for telling the time by looking at the positions of the sun. They should be considered necessary and effective tools in learning and living, used like books, worksheets, manipulatives, balances, compasses, and protractors are now, and like slide rules were in the past.

For some students, the motivation and immediate feedback of computer-managed drill and practice activities will be helpful if used in conjunction with other activities. Graphing calculators that allow for quick connections between equations and graphs, and graphic drawing programs that provide easy depiction, manipulation, and transformation of figures, are particularly useful. Real databanks retrieved from the Internet offer a fine supplement to the data collected by students themselves. Because of the almost universal existence of technology, it is no longer necessary for students to spend time building speed in completing multidigit addition, subtraction, multiplication,

and division algorithms. As soon as the student provides evidence of automaticity in fact retrieval, an understanding of the algorithm strategy, and reasonable accuracy, multidigit problems should be estimated first and then done with a calculator. Some recursive practice with the algorithms can be done from time to time. But we cannot overlook the fact that being able to use technological tools is an important content standard in itself—necessary for survival in the new millennium.

How Teachers Can Use the Following Chapters

A Guide for Writing Grade-Level Curricula

The process standards are not separately presented in Chapter 2 or Chapter 3. Instead, they are embodied continuously in both the content and performance standards within the actions prescribed by such words as *solve, prove, analyze, explain, compare, connect, describe, compute,* and *automaticity,* which are used over and over again in Chapter 2 and in the challenges of the exemplars in Chapter 3. The two listed *disposition or attitude* standards are similarly implied in the real-life applications of Chapter 3 and fostered by the careful attention to conceptual development in Chapter 2. The seven major branches of the *content set* are presented in Chapter 2 in an order that loosely corresponds to the traditional level of concentration on that branch as students progress through the grades. For example, counting is presented first, and the multiple representations of data are at the end. However, each major branch has preparatory concepts at each grade level, so teachers will find concepts for data collection that are appropriate for early grades in the final section. Within the major overlapping branches, each specific minor branch is presented in the order of a presumed developmental sequence.

When preparing grade-level curricula, teachers should go through Chapter 2 and check off all standards appropriate for their own grade level, using the median expectations listed. There may be additional standards that are required by state documents or assessments that need to be considered, as well as some adjustments required by the particular group of students. The order in which the major branches are presented is optional. One branch can be presented at a time, or the teacher may choose to alternate between them. For example, the standards on the rotary clock might be a good introduction to fractions. Another alternative is to follow the order of a textbook, using all sections of this book as a side-by-side accompaniment and day-to-day reference as described below.

A Day-to-Day Reference Guide for Instruction and Informal Assessment

Once the curriculum sequence has been decided upon, teachers may use Chapter 2 as a daily reminder of what students need to know. (For an in-depth discussion on assessment, see Solomon, 1998.) Having the desired concept clearly in mind will help teachers construct planned and unplanned dialogues and activities that meet the needs of each student. The suggestions for scaffolds or instructional mapping dialogue in Chapter 3 will help guide them in this process, but individual students' prior knowledge and motivating goals, as well as the teachers' own experience with successful activities, should be considered. The matching exemplars can be used as they are presented and can also serve as models for the selection or creation of other, similar experiences that will help the student develop a

concept or automate a procedure. The topical index for Chapters 2 and 3 will provide easy access to these for a particular lesson or unit.

The performance standards will delineate clearly the forms and measures of the informal assessments that need to be an integral part of every day's activity because they provide the feedback necessary for reflective practice. Based on the results of these informal assessments, teachers can make day-to-day and moment-to-moment adjustments in their instructional decisions.

Formal Assessments

Formal assessments for the purpose of program evaluation at critical grade benchmarks or at the end of a particular unit of study can be constructed directly from the performance standards in Chapter 2 or from the exemplars in Chapter 3. They may be prepared for analysis and individualized for students in the following manner:

▷ Each item on the assessment (written test or other alternative form) should be articulated with a particular standard by number.

▷ If possible, items should be prepared in multiple forms that reflect the mastery levels. For example, students might be able to solve a problem conceptually with concrete materials or diagrams, but be unable to translate the problem to algorithm form and solve it without materials.

▷ The expected level for each standard should be established. Is the expectation at the exploration level or should the concept mastery or procedural mastery level be reached? Where is each student in reference to this expectation?

▷ An optional, above-standard mastery level, which is not listed in Chapter 2, could be added. This would assume that the student has reached a level of the particular concept where, in addition to solving problems presented by others, the student could create new problems that require that concept or could apply the concept to other contexts or interdisciplinary connections.

▷ When reporting to the students themselves and their parents, the standards should be shared. A report would list the number of the standard and a rubric that corresponds to the three or four developmental levels. The achievement level reached by the student for each standard would be noted, and there would be an indication whether or not that level equaled or exceeded expectation.

A similar standard-by-standard analysis of class means could provide knowledgeable direction for continued group instruction. There are several computer-based management programs that can facilitate each of these analyses and reports. Examples of assessment items matched to standards will be found in Chapter 3. An example of a report to students or parents and a computer-based class analysis will be found in the Resource section.

Note

1. The newly released standards document of the National Council of Teachers of Mathematics (2000) is the basis for the presentation of general standards in this chapter. The presentation differs in its inclusion of standards for perception and attitude. The succinct definitions of embedded terms are elaborated in Chapters 2 and 3. For further elaboration and examples, see the Standards themselves.

CHAPTER 2

Content and Performance Standards

CONTENT AREA BRANCHES		GRADE-LEVEL EXPECTATIONS*			CONTENT STANDARDS— Students Will Know That:	PERFORMANCE STANDARDS— Students Will Demonstrate Their Knowledge By:
Major and Minor		A	B	C		

Number system/counting patterns/algebra
(Language check: Number names, before, after, more, less, larger than, smaller than, total, property, equal to, odd/even)

1.	One-to-one correspondence	K-1	1		Each item touched in sequence corresponds to the next number on the mental number line.	Touching and naming item and identifying position on number line
2.	Cardinal principle	K	1		The last number counted is the group total.	Repeating the last number counted after short interval
3.	Conservation/ number/size	K-1	1	1	Order of counting or arrangement does not affect total number. Spacing of same number of objects does not affect quantity.	Repeating the total in a rearranged set Repeating an equal total quantity when group is expanded
4.	Seriation/ size	K	1	2	Objects can be arranged in size order (increasing and decreasing).	Correct arrangement of objects in size order
5.	Sorting/ classifying	K	1	2-4	Objects can be grouped according to like properties. They can also be put in order according to properties other than size (e.g., lightest to darkest, fastest to slowest).	Identifying property used for correct grouping and class inclusion Logical arrangement of objects based on identified property
6.	Counting: naming, reading, and writing numerals: by (1) up to 20; by (1) to 100	K	K	1	There are patterns: recognition of the "teens" as additions to 10; then, each time you count up to nine, you go on to the next decade.	Correct item counting; touching and naming position on number line; identification of 10 and ___ more for each number to 20; ability to read and write number symbols
7.	Subitizing	K	1	2	You can recognize the totals of small groups of tens (subitize) by looking at them (e.g., three has one in the middle and one on each side, five is made of two and three).	Ability to quickly identify (subitize) totals of small groups (recognize group size on sight)

*NOTE: A = Exploration B = Concept Mastery C = Algorithmic or Procedural Mastery

CONTENT AREA BRANCHES		GRADE-LEVEL EXPECTATIONS*			CONTENT STANDARDS— Students Will Know That:	PERFORMANCE STANDARDS— Students Will Demonstrate Their Knowledge By:
Major and Minor		A	B	C		
8.	Counting: by (10) up to 100	K	1	2	There are patterns in the decades (e.g., the names of the decades [groups of 10] sound like the numbers and "ty"). All numbers end in zero.	Touching and naming decade position on number line; increasing automaticity (fast retrieval from memory)
9.	Counting: by (5) up to 50;	1	1	2	*Skip counting* overlooks a given quantity of numerals in the mental number line. There are patterns in skip counting: by five, all numbers end in five or zero. Counting by two, all numbers are even numbers; the ones in between are odd numbers. Then come doubling patterns. Counting by four skips one of the counts by two: (6) twos are twice as much as (3) twos (see Chapter 3).	Correct skip count explanation; recognition of *patterns*; odd and even numbers; increasing automaticity in counting, matching counted items with symbol, *connecting* patterns to each other
	by (2) up to 20.	1	2	2		
	Odd and even numbers.	1	2	2		
	By (3) up to 36	2	3	3		
	By (4), (6), (8)	3	3	4		
	By (7), (9)	3	4	4		
10.	Algebra: Counting negative and positive integers	5	6	7	We can also think of a number line with values less than zero (e.g., when the temperature is below zero or when you owe money to someone). Values less than zero are negative; values more than zero are positive. The true values of negative numbers decrease as the number name increases. We can call numbers that have value signs integers. There are positive integers, negative integers, and zero, which is neither positive nor negative. We can show negative integers with a high minus sign and positive integers with a high plus or no sign. (The high plus or minus distinguishes it from the operation sign.) (see Chapter 3)	Ability to translate data with negative values to a number line and find the difference between the values

---

*NOTE: A = Exploration B = Concept Mastery C = Algorithmic or Procedural Mastery

CONTENT AREA BRANCHES	GRADE-LEVEL EXPECTATIONS*			CONTENT STANDARDS— Students Will Know That:	PERFORMANCE STANDARDS— Students Will Demonstrate Their Knowledge By:
Major and Minor	A	B	C		
10a. Integer operations: Addition	6	7	8	When integers are added together, one may cancel the other. When combining or adding negative and positive values, the result is the difference between the values. On the number line, we combine numbers by starting at zero and moving one value at a time to the right or left of zero. The final position is the result.	Generalization of the concept that positive and negative values cancel each other when combined or added; proof on the number line or with other data and manipulatives
10b. Integer operations: Subtraction	6	7	8	On the number line, if we count up from ($^-$6) to ($^-$2), we move $^+$4. From this, we can generalize that subtracting a negative integer from a positive or negative integer changes the operation to the addition of a positive integer with the same absolute value. In the subtraction algorithm, we usually start with the higher value and subtract the lower value: ($^-$2) – ($^-$6) = $^+$4. If the subtracted number ($^-$6) is changed to ($^+$6) and the values combined, the result (the difference) is $^+$4.	Generalization of concept that two negatives equal a positive and proof on the number line; proof on number line and with verbal logic; see Chapter 3
11. Ordinality: first to tenth; to twentieth	K 1	1 2	2 3	Ordinal numbers are order dependent. Shifting the order changes the position number, but not the total.	Correct identification of order of given item
12. Place value 1 →100 1 →1,000 1 →10,000 1 →100,000 1 →1,000,000	1 2 2 3 4	1 2 3 4 5	2 3 4 5 6	Our number system is based on 10. There are only 10 symbols for each place 0–9. For higher values, we use the next place to the left. A symbol (1) in the tens place has a value of 10, but (1) in the ones place has a value of 1. *Zero is a placeholder.*	Correct reading and writing of numbers and regrouping of value as separate components of system units (dissembling) (e.g., 107 ones are equal to (1) one hundred, (0) tens, and (7) ones.
13. Systematic equalities; to 99 (100) to 999 (1,000) to 10,000 to 1,000,000	1 1 3 4	1 2 4 5	2 3 5 6	Ten of any units in a place is equal to one in the next higher place (10) ones are equal to (1) ten. (10) tens are equal to (1) hundred. (10) hundreds are equal to (1) thousand. 10,000 = (10) thousands, but it also equals (100) hundreds, etc.	Correct trades with concrete materials; explaining the system generalization; renaming numbers as equal value symbolic alternatives including other multiples of 10 (e.g., 6,000 = 60 hundreds or 600 tens)

---

*NOTE: A = Exploration   B = Concept Mastery   C = Algorithmic or Procedural Mastery

CONTENT AREA BRANCHES	GRADE-LEVEL EXPECTATIONS*			CONTENT STANDARDS— Students Will Know That:	PERFORMANCE STANDARDS— Students Will Demonstrate Their Knowledge By:
Major and Minor	A	B	C		
14. Place value: left and right shift for multiplication and division; by 10, 100 by 1,000	2 3	3 4	4 5	Each digit in a place is 10 times greater than the same digit on its right. Each digit in a place is 10 times smaller than the same digit on its left. You make values 10 times bigger by shifting one place to the left and smaller by shifting one place to the right.	Ability to explain and demonstrate *generalization* by multiplying or dividing any value by 10 and multiples of 10 using right or left shift (at appropriate grade level)
15. Place value: decimals (see #100) to hundredths (to thousandths)	4 5	5 6	5 6	As above, but values less than one are decimals, and we separate the symbols for wholes and decimals with a period or decimal point and the word "and" when reading. The number 25.23 is read "twenty five *and* twenty three one hundredths" (avoid reading "point"). We need zeros for missing digits above the lowest decimal place.	Ability to read combinations of whole numbers and decimals; ability to dissemble (regroup value into separate components) for each place (23.23 = 2 tens, 3 ones, 2 tenths, and 3 one hundredths)
16. Estimation: front-end estimation; rounding numbers one place	2	3	4	It is helpful to estimate numbers to make them easier to communicate and use. Estimates check our calculators. Sometimes, we just look at the largest place value (the front end) and use zero place holders for the lower ones. When rounding numbers, we think about whether the digit in the next lower place is more or less than halfway to the place we want to round to. For rounding to the nearest ten, we know that 5 ones are halfway to one ten, so 5 or more ones are traded for one more ten (round up), and we use zero as a placeholder for the ones. If there are less than 5 ones, we just drop them (round down) and use a zero to hold their place.	Ability to explain the need for estimation and make some judgments on whether front end or rounding is appropriate; use of estimation in conjunction with calculator computation; ability to explain the *generalization* for rounding; correct rounding to next place and use of rounding in estimation
17. Rounding numbers more than one place	3	4	5	Numbers can be rounded to the nearest 100 or thousand, etc. To the nearest hundred, for any value less than 50 or half the hundred, we round down and use zero placeholders; for 50 or more than half the hundred, we round up to the next hundred. To the nearest thousand, we round down for any value less than 500 or half the thousand and up for 500 or more than 500.	Correct rounding to given value (up to values as expected in #13); use of rounding in estimation; ability to explain generalization.

*NOTE: A = Exploration B = Concept Mastery C = Algorithmic or Procedural Mastery

CONTENT AREA BRANCHES	GRADE-LEVEL EXPECTATIONS*			CONTENT STANDARDS—Students Will Know That:	PERFORMANCE STANDARDS—Students Will Demonstrate Their Knowledge By:
Major and Minor	A	B	C		

Operations/patterns: addition, subtraction facts
(Language check: add, subtract, part, whole, combine, separate, symbol compare, difference between, trade)

		A	B	C		
18.	Add and subtract to 10 on a number line counting all	K	1	2	Addition is an increase on the number line, subtraction is a decrease on the number line. The operations can be represented by symbols that stand for the real things (referents). The symbols for the operations are: combining (+) and separating (−).	Correct new number by counting all (CA), up or down when solving change/result unknown problems of given item (see Chapter 3 for sample problems); ability to explain generalization
19.	Add/subtract to 10 on number line, counting from the first number.	K	1	1	It is easier to count from the number that tells where you are on the number line (cardinal principle must be in place) than to count all of the numbers (COF).	Correct new number by counting up from first or counting down from first, in change/result unknown problems (see Chapter 3)
20.	Add to 10 on a number line counting from the larger number. Use choice for subtraction.	1	1	2	It is easier to count from the larger number (COL). For example, in addition, if the problem is 2 + 7, start with the 7. In subtraction, it is sometimes easier to count up (e.g., for 9 − 7, count up from the 7; For 9 − 2, count down). Addends are commutative: 2 + 3 = 3 + 2.	Correct new number for addition by counting from larger number; use of either counting down or counting up—whichever is easier (choice)—in change unknown, result unknown, and start unknown problems
21.	Addition: part/whole recognition	K	1	2	Addition is a combination of parts to form a whole.	Ability to analyze problems and identify parts and whole
22.	Addition/subtraction: related facts/to 18	1	2	3	Whole quantities can be separated into parts. Subtraction is a separation of the parts from the whole. When you put the parts together, you re-form the whole.	Ability to analyze canonical and noncanonical problems (see Chapter 3 for examples); identify parts and whole

---

*NOTE: A = Exploration B = Concept Mastery C = Algorithmic or Procedural Mastery

CONTENT AREA BRANCHES	GRADE-LEVEL EXPECTATIONS*			CONTENT STANDARDS— Students Will Know That:	PERFORMANCE STANDARDS— Students Will Demonstrate Their Knowledge By:
Major and Minor	A	B	C		
23. Equalities of sets; use of = for same as; add to five add to 10	K 1	1 2	2 2	Different combinations of parts can be the same whole: 2 + 3 = 5, 4 + 1 = 5	Recognition of different combinations that are the same whole in equalizing word problems; proof with manipulatives and balances; automatization to 10
24. Addition: three single-digit numbers to 10	1	1	2	More than two parts can be combined to form a whole. They can be combined in any order.	Alternate subtotals when adding three numbers from a story problem
25. Equalities of sets, algebra, associative principle. To total of 10 11-22	1 1	1 2	2 2	We can find a missing addend (part) if we know the whole and the other addend (part): 2 + [ ] = 5. Regrouping values to form 10 can make adding easier (8 + 5 can be regrouped as 8 + 2 + 3). We can describe equal combinations in symbol form.	Proof of associative principle with manipulatives or balance; regrouping to make use of automatization of sums to 10; application to symbolic form
26. Estimation to precision: addition of two-digit numbers to 99—no trading	1	2	3	When adding two-digit numbers, we combine like place value parts (ones to ones, tens to tens). We use symbols in an algorithm to keep track of what we are doing. We can estimate by just adding the tens, but for exact measurement, start with ones.	Correct choice of concrete material and correct placement of two-digit numbers from a story problem, correct estimation and addition using algorithm
27. Addition: three single-digit numbers	1	2	3	It is efficient to look for doubles and to form tens when adding the columns. Ten plus six is 16.	Increased efficiency, evidence of reasoning, in procedures

*NOTE: A = Exploration B = Concept Mastery C = Algorithmic or Procedural Mastery

CONTENT AREA BRANCHES	GRADE-LEVEL EXPECTATIONS*			CONTENT STANDARDS—Students Will Know That:	PERFORMANCE STANDARDS—Students Will Demonstrate Their Knowledge By:
Major and Minor	A	B	C		
28. Addition: three-digit numbers to 999—no trading	2	3	4	Like place value parts are combined. We can estimate by combining the values in the largest place. When adding amounts over 200 and 300, the answer must be at least 500.	Correct choice of concrete materials; correct placement of addends in algorithm from story problems; correct estimates of 100 or more
29. Addition: two-digit numbers with trading; three digits; four digits	1 2 3	2 3 4	3 4 5	Because our number system does not have more than nine units in a place, sums of 10 or more can be renamed as one ten and up to nine ones. (10) tens can be renamed as (1) 100. The addition algorithm helps us keep track of what we are doing.	Correct renaming and correct use of concrete materials; correct transition to symbolic algorithm; proof with materials
30. Addition series: same addend / Increasing addend	2 3	3 4	4 5	We can create number patterns by continuously adding the same number or a number that increases each time.	Ability to recognize addition patterns in series; reasoning with and without concrete materials
31. Subtraction as separation of a part from the whole / One digit from one digit without trading / One digit from two digits	1 1	1 2	2 2	Subtraction finds the value of a part when you know the whole value and the value of another part. In some problems, the part you know is separated from the whole. The part you don't know, or what is left, is the difference between the part you know and the whole. To find the difference, we count up from the part or down from the whole, whichever is easier.	*Analysis of problems:* Identification of whole, known part, and difference sought from real or story problems (comparison, change unknown, start unknown, referent unknown) using real or manipulative materials
32. Subtraction: comparing wholes	1	1	2	Subtraction finds the difference between two whole values. To find the difference, you can count up from the smaller value or down from the larger value, whichever is easier.	Evidence of choice of counting up or down for maximum efficiency

*NOTE: A = Exploration   B = Concept Mastery   C = Algorithmic or Procedural Mastery

CONTENT AREA BRANCHES	GRADE-LEVEL EXPECTATIONS*			CONTENT STANDARDS— Students Will Know That:	PERFORMANCE STANDARDS— Students Will Demonstrate Their Knowledge By:
Major and Minor	A	B	C		
33. Inequalities: use of symbols: < and > Algebra: unequal; unknown numbers that add up to a known whole	1 4	2 5	3 6	Combinations and single amounts can be more or less than each other. Subtraction finds the difference. We can find the value of two unequal numbers we do not know if we know the difference between them and we know their sum. If we subtract the difference between them from the sum, we are left with the sum of two equal values. The value of one of these is the smaller number.	Correct use of terms more, less, same as; then, symbols for these; *analysis and solution* of compare problems Analysis and solution of problems where two parts are unknown, but difference between them and whole is known See Chapter 3
34. Subtraction: two digits from two digits—no trading	1	2	3	Like place value parts must be subtracted from like place value parts.	Correct estimation, then computation with concrete materials; transition to algorithm (see note below)
35. Subtraction: one digit from two digits with trading Two digits from two digits—trading	1 2	1 2	2 3	If we don't have enough of the kind we need, we can *trade* for equal (renamed) quantities. In the problem (23 – 7), 23 is either 2 tens and 3 ones or 1 ten and 13 ones. We can subtract 7 from 13 ones but not from three ones (see Chapter 3 for hints on transition to algorithm).	Correct estimation/correct trading (concrete materials →symbolic algorithm)
36. Three digits from three digits—trading	2	3	4-5	*Trading* can skip places in our number system. It is true that (1) one hundred is the same as 100 ones, but for exact answers, it is better to move one step at a time and not skip places when subtracting across zeros. First, trade the one hundred for (10) tens, and then one ten for ten ones. The place with a zero can be filled by trading larger pieces for those that belong in the place held by zero.	Correct estimation/correct trading across zero; effective and accurate use of subtraction algorithm with three-digit minuend and subtrahend

*NOTE: A = Exploration B = Concept Mastery C = Algorithmic or Procedural Mastery

CONTENT AREA BRANCHES	GRADE-LEVEL EXPECTATIONS*			CONTENT STANDARDS—STUDENTS WILL KNOW THAT:	PERFORMANCE STANDARDS—Students Will Demonstrate Their Knowledge By:
Major and Minor	A	B	C		
37. Subtract: more than three digits—trading	3	4	5	When trading across zeros, it is better to move one step at a time. Use calculator checks.	As above with four digits in all types of word problems and in the common algorithm

Operations/patterns: Multiplication
(Language check: times, as much, double, product, partial product, multiple)

38. Multiplication as repeated addition of groups of size 2 to 5	2	3	4	Every time we skip count, we add another equal amount. *Multiplication is repeated addition.* We keep track of the number of times we have added an equal amount to get a total. "Times" means the number of times a quantity has been repeatedly added. 5 X 1 means 5 added one time, 5 X 2 means 5 added two times, and so on (use arrays and calculators).	Correct analysis of word problems that speak of repeated equal additions (e.g., "Every day of the week, Jon got two new pennies, which he saved. How many times did he receive pennies? How many pennies in all?"); recognition of "groups" and "totals" in arrays
39. Multiplication number sentences in horizontal and vertical forms, multiples of 2, 10, 5, 10	2	3	4	Repeated addition creates patterns, such as twice as many repeats counts up to a double total; 4 X 4 is double 2 X 4 or 4 fours are double 2 fours or twice as much as 8, which is 16.

Measures of standards are repeated addition of units. | Correct analysis of word problems; translation into number sentence and vertical forms |
| 40. Multiplication of groups of size to 10, tables, fact families | 3 | 4 | 5 | We can make a multiplication table to show the patterns of repeated additions. Multiplication by zero means that there is no amount to add. Anything multiplied by zero is zero. | Increasing automaticity of multiplication facts; ability to retrieve facts lost from long-term memory by using analysis and reasoning from known facts |

*NOTE: A = Exploration B = Concept Mastery C = Algorithmic or Procedural Mastery

CONTENT AREA BRANCHES		GRADE-LEVEL EXPECTATIONS*			CONTENT STANDARDS— Students Will Know That:	PERFORMANCE STANDARDS— Students Will Demonstrate Their Knowledge By:
Major and Minor		A	B	C		
41.	Multiplication: commutativity	3	4	5	The sum of a number of groups repeated a certain number of times is the same as the sum you get when a group the same size as the number of times the first group was repeated is repeated a number of times equal to the size of the first group. (See Chapter 3 for clarification of this concept and notation.) 5×3 has the same total as 3×5, but they represent different arrays of things.	Concrete demonstration for proof of commutativity; automaticity in retrieval of commutative facts
42.	Multiplication as comparison or multiple change in size	3	4	5	Multiplication is also a process that changes the value or size of a single object. One balloon can become twice as large or three times bigger, or half as large/half as big (to prepare for multiplication by fractions).	Correct analysis of word problems that address the concept of size change; ability to estimate comparisons in figures
43.	Multiplication patterns: tens, hundreds	4	4	5-6	Using left shift or counting, we know that $10 \times 10 = 100$. But 20×10 is 2 tens $\times$ 1 ten or 200; 20×20 is 2 tens $\times$ 2 tens = 4 hundreds. Then 2 tens $\times$ 2 hundreds is 4 thousands.	Pattern recognition; correct estimation and ability to mentally compute even multiples of tens and hundreds
44.	Multiplication: two-digit multiplicands by single-digit multipliers of 2-10	2	3	4	Like parts need to be multiplied separately, but the sum of partial products equals the whole product (e.g., 23×3 is the same as 20×3 plus 3×3 [distributive principle]). We can estimate answers by multiplying by the tens. Use concrete materials and then transition to algorithm.	Correct estimation and exact answers; identification of the multiplier and repeated groups (multiplicand) in word problems; ability to prove that partial products add up to total
45.	Multiplication: algorithm	3	4	5	The multiplication algorithm organizes the problem and partial products.	Correct estimation and placement of subtotals in algorithm; proof of algorithm strategy
46.	Multiplication: single-digit multipliers and two-digit multiplicands with trading	4	4	5-6	When we organize partial products, we trade values of 10 or more for the next higher place value so that like parts in our number system are combined.	Correct estimation; correct placement of subtotals (partial products) and ability to identify these; correct trading; ability to solve and construct problems

---

*NOTE: A = Exploration B = Concept Mastery C = Algorithmic or Procedural Mastery

CONTENT AREA BRANCHES		GRADE-LEVEL EXPECTATIONS*			CONTENT STANDARDS— Students Will Know That:	PERFORMANCE STANDARDS— Students Will Demonstrate Their Knowledge By:
Major and Minor		A	B	C		
47.	Two-digit multipliers and two-digit multiplicands with trading, using concrete materials and algorithm	3	4	5	In the algorithm 16 × 25, 25 is added repeatedly, first six times, and then 10 times. Use a calculator to demonstrate, following concrete manipulation in which five unit cubes are repeated 16 times and 2 tens blocks are repeated 16 times.	Correct estimation; correct place value of partial products; ability to distribute 16 × 25 as (16 × 20 + 16 × 5) or as (10 × 20 + 10 × 5 + 6 × 20 + 6 × 5)
48.	Multiplication: three-digit multipliers and multiplicands with trading, using algorithm	4	5	6	30 × 200 or 3 tens × 2 hundreds = 6 thousands; 3 hundreds × 2 hundreds = 6 ten thousands. As above for higher multipliers and multiplicands when the total product is the sum of the partial products.	Ability to mentally compute even multiples of hundreds, hundreds of times; 400 × 800 = 320,000; correct estimation and computation with three-digit multiplicands and multipliers; correct use of calculator
49.	Cartesian multiplication: single-chance correspondence	2	3	4	Number patterns can help us compute. If we know the pattern or the relationship, we can compute one number from the other. Diagrams can help us see the patterns. We can also describe the patterns in an equation (an introduction to functions).	Ability to compute a total from the number pattern (e.g., Everyone has two eyes, how many eyes do 5 children have?)
50.	Multiplication series; enlargement by the same multiplier; changing multiplier	5 6	6 7	7 8	If we know the multiplication pattern in a series, we can predict the next number or any future number. Finding common factors (see below) for the numbers helps us see the patterns. The patterns can be expressed in symbol form as a function. For example, for the three table, N = 3 x (n), where (n) stands for the ordinal position of the number in a series and (N) its cardinal value.	Analysis of series; generalization of function and expression in symbolic form

*NOTE: A = Exploration   B = Concept Mastery   C = Algorithmic or Procedural Mastery

CONTENT AREA BRANCHES	GRADE-LEVEL EXPECTATIONS*			CONTENT STANDARDS—Students Will Know That:	PERFORMANCE STANDARDS—Students Will Demonstrate Their Knowledge By:
Major and Minor	A	B	C		

Operations/patterns: Division
(Language checks: divided into, divided by, divisor, dividend, quotient, remainder)

		A	B	C	CONTENT STANDARDS	PERFORMANCE STANDARDS
51.	Division as repeated subtraction; backward skip counting	2	3	4	Skip counting backwards from a whole is repeated subtraction of equal quantities or groups. The groups form equal parts of the whole. (Use calculators to keep track of the number of groups.)	Can orally skip count backwards by 2, 5, 10, and backwards on the calculator while keeping track of number of repetitions
52.	Division as sharing to form equal groups (partition)	2	3	4	Sharing involves forming equal parts or groups from a whole. In sharing division, you know the whole and the number of groups or parts, but not the size of the group or part. With a given whole, the size of the part depends on the number of parts or groups. The larger the number of parts, the smaller the size of each group or part, and vice versa. The size of each group is the answer.	Ability to predict change in size of group with increase or decrease in number of parts; automaticity of responses when given partition problems: "Twenty candies can fill 5 baskets with 4 candies. How many candies could you put in four baskets?" (first more or less as a predictor)
53.	Division: as inversely related to multiplication (quotition)	2	3	4	In multiplication, we know the size of each group and the number of the groups we add repeatedly, but not the size of the whole. We multiply to find the whole. In some division problems, we know the whole and the size of the group, but not the number of groups. We divide to find the number of groups. The answer is called the quotient.	Analysis of word problems to identify what represents the whole, and what represents size of each group; compute and label the number of groups; ability to predict and prove changes in number of groups with increase or decrease in size of group
54.	Division as shrinkage	3	3	4	Division can also be a process in which a whole shrinks a given number of times, such as, What is three times (less) smaller than 12? (related to fractions)	Ability to analyze word problems to identify what represents the original size and compute results of shrinkage in word problems
55.	Division facts, tables; patterns: doubling, halving	3	4	5	Pattern recognition: ▷ If 5 × 6 = 30 and 6 × 5 = 30, then there are five sixes or six fives in 30, 30 ÷ 6 = 5, 30 ÷ 5 = 6. ▷ If there are 3 fours in 12, then there are 6 fours in 24. If there are 4 fives in 20, then there are only 2 fives in 10.	Increasing automaticity with facts and problems involving quotition*; how many groups of 6 are there in 42, etc.? 42 ÷ 6 = ? and 42 ÷ ? = 7; ability to explain canonical and noncanonical sentences *some texts use the term "measurement" division.

*NOTE: A = Exploration   B = Concept Mastery   C = Algorithmic or Procedural Mastery

CONTENT AREA BRANCHES	GRADE-LEVEL EXPECTATIONS*			CONTENT STANDARDS— STUDENTS WILL KNOW THAT:	PERFORMANCE STANDARDS— Students Will Demonstrate Their Knowledge By:
Major and Minor	A	B	C		
56. Division as related to fractions (the sharing model) or partition division	3	4	5	In sharing division, each part is a fraction of the whole. Twenty-eight divided into four parts is the same as $\frac{1}{4}$ of 28 or $\frac{1}{4} \times 28$. In each case, you are looking for the size of the part. $28 \div 4 = \square$; $28 \div \square = 7$; $\frac{1}{4}$ of $28 = \square$; $\frac{1}{4} \times 28 = \square$; $\frac{1}{4}$ of $\square = 7$; $\frac{1}{4} \times \square = 7$	Correct identification of the whole, the number of parts, and what is sought in canonical and noncanonical problem sentences
57. Division facts to 144	3	4	5	Pattern recognition (in addition to reciprocal of multiplication): the number of parts and the size of the parts are commutative. These quantities are called factors of the product. The same product may have other factors for the same whole or product.	Increasing automaticity in retrieval from long-term memory; use of reasoning when lost
58. Division: short-form algorithm; no remainder Short form with remainders	3 4	4 5	5 6	Like place parts must be divided separately. The partial quotients are recorded in the right place. We then find the sum for partial quotients. To divide 44 by 2, 4 tens divided by 2 equals 2 (tens), and 4 ones ÷ 2 = 2 ones, and their sum is 22. Whole values cannot always be divided evenly. Sometimes, there is a remainder. In the algorithm, we can rename remainders to the next smaller place and add them to what is there.	Ability to estimate quotient to nearest ten, identify partial quotients, and parts that have not yet been divided, first in concrete materials, then in the algorithm; correct placement of quotient; explanation of remainders in partial and final quotient Correct use of algorithm
59. Division of three-digit numbers by one-digit number: short and long form, remainders and across zero	4	5	6	The long-form division algorithm helps us keep track of partial products and remainders. Numbers can be renamed and reorganized so that division can be done or made easier. The final quotient is the sum of all of the partial quotients.	Ability to estimate quotients, identify partial quotients, and parts that have not yet been divided (see Chapter 3) Correct use of algorithm

*NOTE: A = Exploration B = Concept Mastery C = Algorithmic or Procedural Mastery

CONTENT AREA BRANCHES	GRADE-LEVEL EXPECTATIONS*			CONTENT STANDARDS—Students Will Know That:	PERFORMANCE STANDARDS—Students Will Demonstrate Their Knowledge By:
Major and Minor	A	B	C		
60. Division by zero	4	5	6	Zero divided into 4 or any number of parts is still zero, and there are zero fours in zero, therefore 0 ÷ 4 = 0. However, the number of zeros in 4 is an undefined amount, therefore 4 ÷ 0 is undefined (see Chapter 3).	Proof of generalization using verbal constructs or materials (sets of data with some zero readings are good to explain undefined amount)
61. Division of three- and four-digit numbers by a two-digit number: long form with remainders and across zero	5	6	7	When dividing by a two-digit number, you are dividing into groups of 20 or 30 (or 2 tens or 3 tens). It is good to estimate first. Hundreds divided by tens are tens, or 6 hundred (600) divided by 2 tens (20) = 3 tens or 30. Thousands divided by tens are hundreds. When doing the algorithm, it is useful to round the divisor down to the digit with the largest place value. If you are dividing by 24 or 26, round to 2 tens. Do not round up (see Chapter 3).	Ability to mentally compute division of multiples of 10 by divisors of 10, 20, 30, 40 (e.g., 200 ÷ 10; 600 ÷ 20; 1,200 ÷ 30; 8,000 ÷ 40); ability to compute exact quotients, identify partial quotients, and remainders for word problems involving two-digit divisors and four-digit dividends (using algorithm)
Number system/patterns/operations: Fractions (Language check: numerator, denominator, equivalent, ratio)					
62. Fractions: equal parts of a whole; unit fraction words and numerals $\frac{1}{2}$, $\frac{1}{4}$	K-1	2	3	Whole things can be equally shared. The whole then becomes parts with special names depending on their size. These names are fractions.	Ability to identify one half of a whole item in a word problem picture
63. Comparing unit fractions Naming numerator and denominator $\frac{1}{2}$, $\frac{1}{3}$, $\frac{1}{4}$, $\frac{1}{5}$, $\frac{1}{8}$, $\frac{1}{10}$	1	2	3	The more parts made out of a whole, the smaller the part. The bottom number of the fraction (denominator) tells you how many parts were made from the whole. The top number (numerator) tells you how many of these parts you are thinking about.	Ability to predict size of a part compared to another, when the number of sharers is known, and recognize number of parts into which the whole has been divided from the fraction name

---

*NOTE: A = Exploration   B = Concept Mastery   C = Algorithmic or Procedural Mastery

CONTENT AREA BRANCHES	GRADE-LEVEL EXPECTATIONS*			CONTENT STANDARDS— STUDENTS WILL KNOW THAT:	PERFORMANCE STANDARDS— Students Will Demonstrate Their Knowledge By:
Major and Minor	A	B	C		
64. Fractions as partition of wholes into parts of wholes; parts equal to whole $\frac{2}{2}$, $\frac{4}{4}$, $\frac{8}{8}$	1	2	3	The total number of parts is equal to the whole. The whole can be expressed as all of the parts in one whole or $\frac{2}{2}$, $\frac{4}{4}$, $\frac{8}{8}$. Less than the total number of parts in one whole is less than a whole. More than the number of parts in one whole is more than one.	Ability to rename $\frac{2}{2}$, $\frac{4}{4}$, $\frac{8}{8}$ as equalities; ability to state as inequalities using <, >, and prove understanding of relationship (e.g., $\frac{2}{2}$ = 1 whole, $\frac{3}{2}$ > 1 whole, $\frac{1}{2}$ < 1 whole)
65. Comparing unit fractions (including inequalities)	2	3	4	Unit fractions of the same whole can be ordered according to their size. The higher the denominator, the smaller the size.	Ability to order unit fractions from symbols
66. Operations on fractions: addition and subtraction of like fractions	2	3	4	Fractions can be combined and separated. If the denominators are the same, the numerators are just added or subtracted. This is because they are like parts.	Ability to analyze and solve simple word problems involving addition or subtraction of fractions with like denominators
67. Fractions: related to division; equal parts of a set; unit fractions	2	3	4	Whole groups of things can also be equally shared and the parts described by fractions. This is like division, but the fraction name tells you only how many parts—not how many in each part. The actual size of the part or group depends on the size of the whole. You have to divide by the denominator to find the size of one part.	Ability to use a fraction to describe a part from a number story; ability to predict comparative size of equal unit fractions of different wholes ($\frac{1}{2}$ of 20 vs. $\frac{1}{2}$ of 40); ability to compute size of part for unit fractions
68. Fractions as shrinkage	2	3	4	Fractions are used to describe how much smaller a size or value is compared to another (e.g., half as many).	Ability to estimate half-size shrinkage from diagrams, real objects; use fractions to describe comparison figures

*NOTE: A = Exploration   B = Concept Mastery   C = Algorithmic or Procedural Mastery

CONTENT AREA BRANCHES	GRADE-LEVEL EXPECTATIONS*			CONTENT STANDARDS— Students Will Know That:	PERFORMANCE STANDARDS— Students Will Demonstrate Their Knowledge By:
Major and Minor	A	B	C		
69. Fractions: more than unit fractional parts of a set	4	5	6	To find the size of more than one unit fraction of a set, you find the size of one unit by dividing by the denominator and then multiplying by the number of unit parts, or the numerator.	Ability to compute the value of more than unit fractional parts of multiple wholes from story problems
70. Fractions as sharing of more than one whole where the number of parts is greater than the number of wholes	4	5	6	If you divide two wholes into three parts, the size of each part is less than one whole or $\frac{1}{3}$ of one whole plus $\frac{1}{3}$ of the other or $\frac{2}{3}$ can mean two wholes divided into three parts. A fraction is another way of expressing division.	Ability to form fractions from division number stories; ability to predict whether the size of the part is smaller or greater than one whole
71. Fractions: simple equivalents: halves, fourths Thirds, sixths, fifths, tenths	1 2	2 3	3 4	Equal parts can be combined to form larger equal parts, or smaller equal parts can be formed from larger parts. The smaller the part, the more parts you need to have the same amount of a whole. The higher the denominator, the smaller the part and the more parts you need to have the same amount of the whole (use concrete pieces and fraction number lines).	Ability to identify equivalents and predict whether or not numerators or denominators will be higher or lower (e.g., $\frac{1}{2} = \frac{?}{4}$ [higher or lower than one?])
72. Comparing equivalent fractions Using patterns to compute equivalents	4 5	5 6	6 7	Equivalent fractions have observable patterns. For example, if the numerator is twice as large, the denominator is twice as large ($\frac{2}{3} = \frac{4}{6}$). We can use this pattern to find equivalents by multiplying or dividing numerator and denominator by the same value.	Ability to identify patterns and use them to compute equivalents
73. Fractions as ratios	3	4-5	5-6	Fractions can also be seen as patterns that help us compute totals. Five out of 10 parts is the same as one out of two parts, or half the total number of parts.	Ability to analyze word problems and compute unknown quantities from the ratio pattern; interpretation of scale drawings at Grade 5

*NOTE: A = Exploration B = Concept Mastery C = Algorithmic or Procedural Mastery

CONTENT AREA BRANCHES		GRADE-LEVEL EXPECTATIONS*			CONTENT STANDARDS— Students Will Know That:	PERFORMANCE STANDARDS— Students Will Demonstrate Their Knowledge By:
Major and Minor		A	B	C		
74.	Inequalities, halves, thirds, fourths $\frac{3}{4} > \frac{1}{2}$ $\frac{1}{2} > \frac{1}{3}$ Ordering by other comparisons	4 5	5 6	6 7	If fractions are not equivalent, you can use close equivalents to estimate their relative size (e.g., $\frac{3}{4}$ is more than $\frac{1}{2}$ because $\frac{1}{2}$ is equivalent to $\frac{2}{4}$). Or compare to one whole: $\frac{7}{8}$ is more than $\frac{5}{7}$ because it is only $\frac{1}{8}$ less than whole. (Use fraction number lines and concrete materials.)	Ability to order halves, thirds, fourths, and solve inequalities; $\frac{1}{2} < \frac{3}{4}$; $\frac{1}{2} < \frac{2}{3}$; $\frac{2}{3} < \frac{3}{4}$; $\frac{1}{3} < \frac{1}{2}$; ability to order other fractions without converting to equal denominators

Multiplicative functions/algebra fractions

(Language check: referent, multiple, increment, operator, factor, least common factor, and least common multiple; proper and improper fractions)

		A	B	C		
75.	Preparation for multiple factors: associative principle	5	6	7	The multiplication process is one in which a value is either added or changed in size repeatedly. The multiplier tells how many repeats or what change in size. If the original value or referent is multiplied over and over in separate steps or increments, and each time it is the previous product that is multiplied, the same end result can be obtained by multiplying the original referent by the product of each incremental step (see Chapter 3).	Ability to analyze word problems and identify the referent and abstract operator (multiplier); ability to provide alternate increments for reaching the same enlargement or repeated addition
76.	Factors	5	6	7	Factors are all of the whole number values (referent and abstract operators) that can be combined in the multiplication process to give a particular value of the product. Dividing a whole by one factor results in another factor.	Ability to identify all factors in a given number; given a number and a factor, identify other factors; identify quotient and dividends as factors
77.	Multiples	5	6	7	Multiples are the products of factors.	Use of the term multiple in framing a problem
78.	Prime number	5	6	7	A prime number is a whole number with only 2 factors: itself and 1.	Ability to identify a prime number and prove what it is
79.	Composite numbers	5	6	7	A composite number is a whole number that has more than two factors.	Ability to identify a composite number and prove it

---

*NOTE: A = Exploration B = Concept Mastery C = Algorithmic or Procedural Mastery

CONTENT AREA BRANCHES	GRADE-LEVEL EXPECTATIONS*			CONTENT STANDARDS— Students Will Know That:	PERFORMANCE STANDARDS— Students Will Demonstrate Their Knowledge By:
Major and Minor	A	B	C		
80. Common multiples	5	6	7	Common multiples are computed new multiple values that are the same for two different starting numbers. A balloon of size four blown up three whole times will be the same size as a balloon of size three blown up four times. Both balloons will now be size 12. So will a balloon of size 2 blown up six times, and so on. Twelve is a common multiple of the different numbers 3, 4, 2, 6, 12, and 1.	Ability to identify the common multiples of two or more numbers and prove them
81. Common factors	5	6	7	Common factors are whole number quotients that are the same for different starting numbers. See Chapter 3 for scaffolds and illustrations.	Ability to explain meaning of common factors, and identify common factors of two or more numbers and prove them correct
82. Least common multiple	5	6	7	The least common multiple (LCM) is the smallest value that is a multiple of each of two or more different values. If both values are prime numbers, then the LCM is the product of the two different values. If both values share common factors, the least common multiple will be less than their product.	Ability to predict and compute the least common multiple for different values
83. Greatest common factor	5	6	7	The greatest common factor (GCF) is the largest factor that is common (or the same) for two different numbers.	Ability to define, explain, predict, and compute the greatest common factor
84. Finding equivalent fractions	5	6	7	If we enlarge or reduce the numerator of a fraction by multiplying or dividing it by a value, we can form an equivalent fraction by multiplying or dividing the denominator by the same value. 3/4 is equal to 6/8 because $3 \times (2) = 6$ and $4 \times (2) = 8$, and two is the value by which both numerator and denominator were enlarged. The greater the denominator, the smaller the size of each part, and the more parts necessary for an equivalent fraction. Parts that are twice as small require twice as many parts to be equivalent.	Explanation of generalization; proof that value is not changed (use manipulatives); ability to change fractions to equivalents with common denominators

*NOTE: A = Exploration B = Concept Mastery C = Algorithmic or Procedural Mastery

CONTENT AREA BRANCHES	GRADE-LEVEL EXPECTATIONS*			CONTENT STANDARDS—Students Will Know That:	PERFORMANCE STANDARDS—Students Will Demonstrate Their Knowledge By:
Major and Minor	A	B	C		
85. Least common denominator: changing fractions with unequal denominators to equivalents with equal denominators	5	6	7	In order to perform operations on unlike fractions, we have to change them to equivalents with a common denominator. The least common denominator of a group of fractions is the least common multiple of all of the denominators. We can find the least common denominator for groups of fractions by multiplying (or dividing) the numerator and the denominator of a fraction by the same number because this does not change its value. See Chapter 3 for suggestions for calculator use.	Ability to identify common denominators for fractions such as halves, fourths, eighths, thirds, sixths, tenths, and twelfths
86. Addition and subtraction of unlike fractions with horizontal and vertical representation of fraction problems. Without trading; With trading from whole numbers	5 6	6 7	7 8	Unlike fractions cannot be added or subtracted before they are put into equivalent form with a common denominator. Once they have a common denominator, they can be added or subtracted by combining or finding the difference in the numerators. Trading from whole numbers to equivalent fractions allows us to solve some addition and subtraction fraction problems.	Ability to add and subtract unlike fractions (as above) without trading Ability to add and subtract unlike fractions (as above) with trading (use of algorithm)
87. The division meaning of fractions (more conceptual review)	6	7	8	The fraction form also represents the division operation. One half is one whole divided by two and $4/2 = 4 \div 2$. We can express any division problem with a fraction or change a fraction into a division problem and get a quotient. This helps with unequal denominators.	Ability to translate division problems and statements to fraction form and find quotients for fractions; use of calculator to get decimal value of fractions

---

*NOTE: A = Exploration B = Concept Mastery C = Algorithmic or Procedural Mastery

CONTENT AREA BRANCHES		GRADE-LEVEL EXPECTATIONS[a]			CONTENT STANDARDS— STUDENTS WILL KNOW THAT:	PERFORMANCE STANDARDS— Students Will Demonstrate Their Knowledge By:
Major and Minor		A	B	C		
88.	Renaming fractions that have values greater than 1 (improper fractions)	4	5	6	Fractions that have values greater than 1 can be changed to mixed numbers; and mixed numbers to fractions with values greater than 1. They are different symbols for the same value.	Ability to interchange the symbol forms of equally valued numbers
89.	Multiplication of fractions by whole numbers	4	5	6	When a fraction is multiplied by a whole number, the fraction is repeatedly added or changed a whole number of times. The product is a fraction whose numerator is the product of the original numerator and the whole number abstract operator (multiplier) and whose denominator is the same as the repeated fraction (multiplicand).	Ability to analyze and solve problems that require multiplication of fractions by whole numbers using conceptually repeated additions
90.	Multiplication of whole numbers by fractions	5	6	7	When a whole number is multiplied by a fraction, it is the same as finding the fractional part of the whole number or set. $\frac{1}{2} \times 12$ is the same as $\frac{1}{2}$ of 12 because it means taking the whole only a half of a time.	Ability to analyze and solve problems that require the multiplication of whole numbers by fractions using conceptually repeated additions
91.	Predicting products of fractional multiples of fractions	5	6	7	The product of a value multiplied by a fraction less than a whole is always less than the value. When a fraction is multiplied by a fraction, it is the same as finding the fractional part of the fraction. $\frac{1}{2}$ times $\frac{1}{4} = \frac{1}{8}$ or $\frac{1}{2}$ of $\frac{1}{4}$ is $\frac{1}{8}$.	Ability to predict whether the product of a value and a fraction will be more or less than the value; prove this with fraction bars
92.	Using number sense to compute fractional multiples of fractions	5	6	7	$\frac{1}{2}$ of $\frac{2}{3}$ is going to be $\frac{1}{3}$ $\frac{1}{3}$ of $\frac{3}{4}$ is $\frac{1}{4}$ $\frac{1}{2} \times \frac{1}{40}$ is $\frac{1}{80}$ $\frac{1}{5} \times \frac{5}{6}$ is $\frac{1}{6}$ $\frac{1}{2}$ of $2\frac{1}{2}$ is $1\frac{1}{4}$.	Ability to mentally compute some obvious fractional multiples of fractions

*NOTE: A = Exploration   B = Concept Mastery   C = Algorithmic or Procedural Mastery

CONTENT AREA BRANCHES		GRADE-LEVEL EXPECTATIONS*			CONTENT STANDARDS—Students Will Know That:	PERFORMANCE STANDARDS—Students Will Demonstrate Their Knowledge By:
Major and Minor		A	B	C		
93.	Unit fractions of unit fractions; unit fractions of more than unit fractions; multiplication of fractions algorithm	6	7	8	Finding a unit fractional part of a unit fraction value (or multiplying the value by the fraction as above) has the same effect as dividing the value by the denominator of the unit fractional part. It makes the value that much smaller. $\frac{1}{4}$ of $\frac{1}{5}$ is going to be four times smaller than $\frac{1}{5}$. $\frac{1}{5}$ will be divided into four smaller parts and each part will only be $\frac{1}{20}$. You can see that the computed value has a denominator that is the product of the two denominators. $\frac{1}{3}$ of $\frac{1}{7}$ would be $\frac{1}{21}$, but $\frac{1}{3}$ of $\frac{2}{7}$ is twice as much, or $\frac{2}{21}$. You can see that for this problem, it was also necessary to multiply the numerators. A shortcut algorithm strategy is just to multiply the numerators and denominators.	Ability to explain why multiplying a unit fraction by a unit fraction results in a product of smaller value, and why the product is a fraction with a denominator that is the product of the two denominators and a numerator of one; ability to explain algorithm and compute unit fractions of fractions (see Chapter 3)
94.	More than unit fractions; of unit fractions; of more than unit fractions	6	7	8	To find more than one unit fraction of a unit fraction, you can find the smaller unit fraction value by multiplying the denominators; then, because it is more than one unit, multiply the numerators. $\frac{2}{3}$ of $\frac{1}{2} = \frac{2}{6}$ because $\frac{1}{3}$ of $\frac{1}{2} = \frac{1}{6}$ and $\frac{2}{3}$ is twice as much as $\frac{1}{3}$ of $\frac{1}{2}$. The shortcut procedure is to multiply numerators and denominators.	Ability to explain and apply the multiplication of fractions algorithm; ability to analyze fraction of fraction problems
95.	Lowest terms	4	5	6	In order to make our mathematical language and operations simpler, we often change fractions to their equivalents with the smallest denominator. We know that dividing the numerator and denominator by the same value does not change the value, and so we try to find the largest value by which we can divide both numerator and denominator.	Correct computation of lowest-term equivalents (*Note: Do not belabor this if it is not specifically required, but it will sometimes be necessary to explain differences between invented strategies and algorithms. For example, it is easy to understand that half of $\frac{2}{3}$ is $\frac{1}{3}$, but if you use the algorithm, you have to change $\frac{2}{6}$ to $\frac{1}{3}$.*)

*NOTE: A = Exploration   B = Concept Mastery   C = Algorithmic or Procedural Mastery

CONTENT AREA BRANCHES	GRADE-LEVEL EXPECTATIONS*			CONTENT STANDARDS— Students Will Know That:	PERFORMANCE STANDARDS— Students Will Demonstrate Their Knowledge By:
Major and Minor	A	B	C		
96. Division of fractions by whole numbers	6	7	8	Division of fractions by whole numbers is like division of whole numbers. We know the size of the whole, and we look either for the number of parts or the size of the parts. In partition, ¾ divided by 3 means if I divide ¾ into 3 parts, how big will each part be? (¼). In quotition, it means how many parts of size (3) are there in ¾? There is less than one part of size 3 in ¾. There is only ¼ of a part of size 3 in ¾. In both cases, ¾ ÷ 3 = ¼.	Ability to demonstrate the division of a fraction by a whole number using fraction bars or other objects; ability to identify divisor and dividend from a division of fraction problem and tell what the quotient represents; ability to mentally compute exemplars of the process
97. Division of fractions and whole numbers by fractions	6	7	8	Division of whole numbers and fractions by fractions is somewhat different in that only quotition problems can be explained easily. 3 ÷ ½ means how many ½-size parts are there in 3? (6). ¾ ÷ ¼ means how many ¼-size parts are there in ¾? (3)	Ability to demonstrate the division of a whole number or a fraction by a fraction using fraction bars or other objects; ability to identify divisor and dividend from a division-by-fraction problem and tell what the quotient represents
98. Division of fractions using algorithm	6	7	8	To divide by a fraction, we can just invert the divisor and then multiply the dividend and the divisor (see Chapter 3).	Ability to use the division-by-fractions algorithm

Number system/operations/patterns/decimals
(Language check: tenths, hundredths, etc.; decimal point)

CONTENT AREA BRANCHES	A	B	C	CONTENT STANDARDS	PERFORMANCE STANDARDS
99. Using decimals for money	2	3	4	Money is made up of dollars and cents. A dollar can be traded for 100 cents. We write the symbols for cents after a decimal point to show that it is less than a dollar. One hundred cents is always written as a whole dollar and zero cents. The dollar sign is also used.	Ability to transcribe word sentences to symbols for dollars and cents
100. Decimals as an alternate form of common fractions: (a) tenths (b) hundredths	3 4	4 5	5 6	The fractions one tenth and one hundredth can be written as decimal fractions or parts less than one whole by placing a decimal point after the smallest whole numeral place (the ones place). One tenth is one tenth of one whole. One hundredth is one tenth of one tenth or one hundredth of a whole. The zero is used as a placeholder to tell .2 from .02.	Ability to symbolically rename tenths and hundredths in decimal form; ability to compare relative decimal and whole numbers in inequalities: 2 > .2 .2 > .02

*NOTE: A = Exploration   B = Concept Mastery   C = Algorithmic or Procedural Mastery

CONTENT AREA BRANCHES		GRADE-LEVEL EXPECTATIONS*			CONTENT STANDARDS— Students Will Know That:	PERFORMANCE STANDARDS— Students Will Demonstrate Their Knowledge By:
Major and Minor		A	B	C		
101.	Comparing and ordering decimals (a) tenths (b) hundredths	3 4	4 5	5 6	Decimals can be renamed. Fifteen hundredths is the same as one tenth and 5 hundredths. One tenth is the same as ten one hundredths and more than nine one hundredths.	Ability to order tenths and hundredths
102.	Rounding decimals to whole numbers	4	5	6	Sometimes, we need only whole numbers. Five tenths or more (½ or more) is usually rounded to the next whole number; less than .5 or ½ to the lower whole number.	Ability to round off to whole numbers from tenths
103.	Place value system connections: right and left shift for multiplication and division by whole multiples of 10	4	5	6	Each digit in a decimal place is 10 times larger than the same digit in a place on its right and 10 times smaller than one on its left. To make a decimal value 10 times larger, shift it one place to the left; to make it 10 times smaller (divide it by 10), shift it to the right.	Ability to multiply and divide any decimal number by 10 or 100 mentally by shifting place (Note: Students may also choose the alternative of moving the decimal point, but only after understanding the connection to place value)
104.	Addition-subtraction: tenths hundredths thousandths	3 4 5	4 5 6	5 6 7	Decimals can be added and subtracted like whole numbers, but like denominations must be added or trading must be done; for example, five tenths can be subtracted from 1 whole if the whole is traded for 10 tenths. Ten hundredths = 1 tenth Ten thousandths equals 1 hundredth Thousandths are one tenth as large as hundredths.	Ability to estimate and add and/or subtract decimals to tenths, hundredths; ability to rename ones, tens, and hundredths as thousandths (decimal and common fraction)
105.	Decimal parts of an area	4	5	6	Parts of a whole or area can be renamed as decimal parts.	Ability to describe parts of an area in decimal terms

---

*NOTE: A = Exploration B = Concept Mastery C = Algorithmic or Procedural Mastery

CONTENT AREA BRANCHES		GRADE-LEVEL EXPECTATIONS*			CONTENT STANDARDS— Students Will Know That:	PERFORMANCE STANDARDS— Students Will Demonstrate Their Knowledge By:
Major and Minor		A	B	C		
106.	Multiplication of decimals: concept ideas, whole numbers by tenths	5	6	7	Multiplying by a decimal is like multiplying by a fraction. The product of any number multiplied by a decimal is going to have a lesser value than the original number. Multiplying a whole number by $\frac{1}{10}$ or .1 results in the same value as dividing it by 10. Multiplying it by .2 is like multiplying it by $\frac{2}{10}$; you multiply by two and divide by 10; .5 times a number is the same as $\frac{5}{10}$ or $\frac{1}{2}$ times the number.	Ability to estimate multiplication of whole numbers by decimals; ability to compute products
107.	Multiplication by two place decimals with trading; multiplication algorithm	6	7	8	One tenth times one tenth is one hundredth (.1 X .1 = .01) because $\frac{1}{10}$ of $\frac{1}{10}$ is $\frac{1}{100}$. Tenths X units = tenths, tenths X hundredths = thousandths.	Correct computation using algorithm; analysis and solution of problems; correct placement of decimal points
108.	Percentage	5	6	7	A common use of decimal fractions is percentage. Parts of a whole value are expressed in hundredths. Percent means parts of one hundred. 25% is the same as $\frac{25}{100}$ or $\frac{1}{4}$. If the percent is less than 100%, the value will be less; 100% of a value is the same as the value; and more than 100% of a value is more than the value.	Ability to change percentages to decimals and common fractions; ability to estimate percentages of whole values, especially more or less than value
109.	Finding percentages 10% and 1% other percentages	5 6	6 7	7 8	We can find 10% or $\frac{10}{100}$ or $\frac{1}{10}$ of a value by shifting the whole value to the next smaller place. One percent of a number is the whole value shifted two places to the right (or move the decimal point to the left to accomplish the same thing). Even multiples of 10% or 1% can also be computed mentally. For other percentages, change the percentage to a decimal and multiply the whole number by it.	Ability to mentally compute 10% and 1% of a number; ability to mentally compute 20% and 2% of a number, and so on; ability to compute a percent of a number by changing to decimal and multiplying

*NOTE: A = Exploration B = Concept Mastery C = Algorithmic or Procedural Mastery

CONTENT AREA BRANCHES	GRADE-LEVEL EXPECTATIONS*			CONTENT STANDARDS— Students Will Know That:	PERFORMANCE STANDARDS— Students Will Demonstrate Their Knowledge By:
Major and Minor	A	B	C		
110. Division of decimals	6	7	8	For exact division of decimals by whole numbers 10, 100, and 1,000, you can use a right place position shift. We get quotients more than one whole when we divide a whole number or a decimal fraction by a smaller valued decimal or fraction. We get quotients less than one whole when we divide a whole number or a decimal number by a value that is larger (e.g., 2.5 ÷ 1.2 is going to be more than one whole or about 2).	Ability to divide or shrink decimals by multiples of 10 using a right shift of place position; ability to conceptually estimate quotients for problems with one digit decimal divisors, and ability to predict whether answers will be more or less than one
111. Dividing decimals: eliminating decimals by equal multiplication of numerator and denominator or dividend and divisor	6	7	8	Dividing .8 by .2 is the same as dividing 8 by 2 or 80 by 20, or 800 by 200. Then, 2.4 divided by 1.2 is the same as 24 ÷ 12. We can eliminate decimals and get the correct answer using the division algorithm if we multiply dividend and divisor by the same multiplier or enlarge them both the same amount (connect to common fraction equivalents).	Ability to convert decimal divisors to whole numbers by equal enlargement of divisor and dividend; ability to explain and apply division algorithm; ability to use calculator to compute exact answers for decimal division problems with higher values

Measurement/Patterns/Operations:
(Language check: same as, more, less, shorter than, longer than, heavier than, wider than, holds more than, object/property/attribute, unit, standard/non-standard, customary, metric, square unit, mass/weight)

CONTENT AREA BRANCHES				CONTENT STANDARDS	PERFORMANCE STANDARDS
112. Vocabulary of measure equalities	K	1	2	Different words help us describe and compare objects so that we can communicate about them. These are measures.	Ability to match descriptive measure words and real objects or pictures
113. Nonstandard units of measures as equalities	K	1	2	We can use things we know to help us measure things for which we don't know the size. We know how big a block is, and we can measure our desks with blocks. We must be careful not to leave spaces.	Ability to estimate and make measurements expressed in nonstandard units as equalities

*NOTE: A = Exploration B = Concept Mastery C = Algorithmic or Procedural Mastery

CONTENT AREA BRANCHES	GRADE-LEVEL EXPECTATIONS*			CONTENT STANDARDS— Students Will Know That:	PERFORMANCE STANDARDS— Students Will Demonstrate Their Knowledge By:
Major and Minor	A	B	C		

Length: area, perimeter (Language check: inch, foot, yard, centimeter, meter, millimeter)

CONTENT AREA BRANCHES	A	B	C	CONTENT STANDARDS	PERFORMANCE STANDARDS
114. Estimating and measuring in nonstandard units	1	2	3	This is the same as above, but using increased precision for length and expressed as inequalities (e.g., the desk is more than five hands long).	Ability to measure using nonstandard units with some precision; ability to express equalities and inequalities
115. Estimating and measuring in: whole feet, inches, yards, whole centimeters, whole meters, millimeters	1 2 1 2 3	2 3 2 3 4	3 4 3 3 5	The centimeter and the inch are standard measures. Standard measures are useful because everyone's hand or foot is different. Governments decide standards. Items measured with these units will always be the same measured length and understood by others. The standards have special names and abbreviations.	Ability to estimate the size of common objects using metric and customary standards alternately; ability to measure using these units; ability to record measures using appropriate units and abbreviations
116. Standard equivalents customary; metric	2 3	3 4	4 5	Standard units can be combined into larger units. The equivalents are also standards. Larger units are better for measuring larger objects or spaces. The larger the unit size, the fewer the number of units. For example: 1 foot = 12 inches, 3 feet = 1 yard; 100 cm = 1 m, 1 cm = 10 mm; 5,280 feet = 1 mile.	Ability to describe standard equivalents in same system from larger to smaller and vice versa; ability to justify use of larger or smaller unit; ability to connect measures to real-life applications
117. Equivalent measures: feet, yards, miles; m, cm, km	2 3	3 4	4 5	To convert measurements from the smaller size unit to the larger, you divide by the standard equivalent; to convert from the larger size unit to the smaller, you multiply by the equivalent. Metric conversions can be made by multiplying or dividing by multiples of 10. Remainders are the smaller unit.	Ability to explain conversion generalization; ability to convert metric and customary measurements from smaller to larger and larger to smaller units: m, cm, km, mm; in, ft, yd
118. Equivalent measures: customary system conversions	3	4	5	A meter is a little more than 3 feet. There are about 2½ cm in an inch, and a little more than 2 km in a mile.	Ability to estimate metric and customary equivalents

*NOTE: A = Exploration B = Concept Mastery C = Algorithmic or Procedural Mastery

CONTENT AREA BRANCHES		GRADE-LEVEL EXPECTATIONS*			CONTENT STANDARDS— Students Will Know That:	PERFORMANCE STANDARDS— Students Will Demonstrate Their Knowledge By:
Major and Minor		A	B	C		
119.	Estimating and measuring perimeter in inches and centimeters; square, rectangle, triangle; pentagon, hexagon	2 3	3 4	4 5	The perimeter of an object is the distance around its edges. Distance tells how far you must go to walk around the edge. We add all of the separate measures to find the total.	Ability to estimate and solve real-life word problems (e.g., fencing) and diagrams for finding perimeter Use of geoboards in providing solutions
120.	Estimating and measuring area (square and rectangle)	3	4	5	Area is the amount of space on a flat surface as measured by square units (or the amount of square units needed to cover it). Multiplication is a shortcut for adding repeated similar groups of square units (use geoboards and centimeter graph paper).	Ability to define a square unit and to use a grid to measure area; ability to write multiplication sentences for repeated similar groups
121.	Area of a right triangle	5	6	7	Not all areas have repeated similar groups of units, but we can use our geometric knowledge to help us measure these areas. The area of a right triangle is half the area of a rectangle that can be formed by putting together two of the same right triangles.	Ability to describe how the area of the right triangle is half the area of the rectangle formed; ability to compute area of given right triangle
Mass/Weight *(Language check: ounce, pound, ton, gram, kg., mass, weight, balance) Note: Use the term weight until grade three or four and then begin to use the term mass as an alternate with the understanding that weight depends on gravity but mass is independent (our weights are different on the moon and Mars but our masses are the same).*						
122.	Finding mass in nonstandard units	2	3	4	We use what we know (coins, washers, cubes) to weigh and compare what we do not know. Balances help us measure weight; equal weights balance.	Ability to use balance to measure unknowns in nonstandard units
123.	Ordering of mass in nonstandard units	2	3	4	The larger the mass (weight) of an object, the greater the number of nonstandard units.	Ability to estimate and order mass quantities when compared to nonstandard units

*NOTE: A = Exploration B = Concept Mastery C = Algorithmic or Procedural Mastery

CONTENT AREA BRANCHES		GRADE-LEVEL EXPECTATIONS			CONTENT STANDARDS— STUDENTS WILL KNOW THAT:	PERFORMANCE STANDARDS— Students Will Demonstrate Their Knowledge By:
Major and Minor		A	B	C		
124.	Reading scales and balances	3	4	5	A bathroom or butcher's scale has a spring instead of standard weights. The standard is in the give of the spring; heavier weights pull the spring more (use spring scales).	Ability to predict relative give of spring for different standard weights; accurate use of the balance and spring scale
125.	Comparing mass of familiar objects to standards: 1 kg, 1 lb.	2	3	4	The standards of measure for mass (use weight until grade 4) is the pound (lb) or kilogram (kg). A pound is about the weight of a large bag of M&Ms. A kilogram is a little more than the weight of two bags (see Chapter 3).	Ability to name standard and abbreviation, estimate weight based on pound or kilogram standard; compare pound and kilogram as an inequality
126.	Measuring mass in ounces and pounds; grams and kilograms	3	4	5	The mass of an object can be determined by comparing it to standard units of grams, kilograms, and pounds.	Ability to estimate and order measured masses; prove them with the balance
127.	Equivalent standards	4	5	6	Standard units can be combined into larger units. The equivalent heavier units are better for measuring heavier objects. The larger the unit size, the fewer the number of units. For example: 16 oz. = 1 lb., 1 ton = 2,000 lbs., 1,000 gm. = 1 kg.	Ability to explain conversion generalization; ability to describe metric and customary standards for units and change from smaller to larger and larger to smaller units
128.	Equivalent standard conversions: oz.↔lbs.↔tons, kg↔gm↔mg	6	7	8	To convert from the smaller size unit to the larger, you divide by the standard; to convert from the larger size unit to the smaller, you multiply. The larger the unit size, the fewer the number of units. We can use function equations: (oz.) = $16 \times$ (lbs.), (lbs.) = (oz.) $\div$ 16. For metrics, conversions can be made by multiplying or dividing by multiples of 10: (# of gm) = $1,000 \times$ (# of kg), (# of kg) = (# of gm) $\div$ 1,000.	Ability to make exact correct equivalent conversions from grams to kilograms or ounces to pounds using equations; solve problems that require it

*NOTE: A = Exploration B = Concept Mastery C = Algorithmic or Procedural Mastery

CONTENT AREA BRANCHES	GRADE-LEVEL EXPECTATIONS*			CONTENT STANDARDS— Students Will Know That:	PERFORMANCE STANDARDS— Students Will Demonstrate Their Knowledge By:
Major and Minor	A	B	C		
129. Conversions between different standard systems	6	7	8	A kilogram is a little more than 2 lbs.	Correct estimations from metric to English (customary) standards and exact conversions with a calculator

Capacity/Volume
(Capacity is usually applied to liquids and small particle solids because they fill their containers. Volume is applied to rigid objects that do not fill containers.)

CONTENT AREA BRANCHES	GRADE-LEVEL EXPECTATIONS*			CONTENT STANDARDS— Students Will Know That:	PERFORMANCE STANDARDS— Students Will Demonstrate Their Knowledge By:
130. Conservation of capacity	K	1	2	The shape of a container does not determine its capacity. Equal amounts of liquid can look different in different containers, but there is no loss of quantity when containers are changed.	Ability to correctly judge Piagetian conservation tasks
131. Estimating and comparing (capacity)	1	2	3	Different-sized containers have different capacities. A full container of liquid will not fill a larger container.	Ability to predict whether or not a container will be filled; capacity expressed as equalities and inequalities
132. Standard units of cups, pints, quarts, liters	2 / 4	3 / 5	4 / 6	Standards of capacity help us measure more exactly. We measure liquids by pouring the liquid into the standard.	Estimation of capacity; ability to measure by pouring liquid into standard and recording
133. Equivalent conversions: as above for milliliters, liters	3 / 4	4 / 5	5 / 6	Equations describe conversions: 1 cup = 16 fluid ounces, 2 cups = 1 pint, 4 quarts = 1 gallon, 2 pints = 1 quart = 4 half-pints, 2 quarts = 1 half-gallon. 1 liter = 1000 milliliters.	Ability to solve problems that require equivalent conversions including quart to liter and liter to gallon
134. Customary system conversions	4	5	6	A quart is just a little less than a liter. A half-gallon or 2-quart milk container is less than a 2-liter soda. Estimate only, or use a calculator.	Ability to solve problems that require conversions

*NOTE: A = Exploration B = Concept Mastery C = Algorithmic or Procedural Mastery

▶ 43

CONTENT AREA BRANCHES	GRADE-LEVEL EXPECTATIONS*			CONTENT STANDARDS— Students Will Know That:	PERFORMANCE STANDARDS— Students Will Demonstrate Their Knowledge By:
Major and Minor	A	B	C		
135. Estimating volume; counting cubes to find volume (nonstandard units)	3	4	5	Volume is the amount of space taken up by solid (3-D) objects. We measure volume by adding up cubes as units. Structures of varying volumes can be built on the same area. The metric standard unit of volume is the cubic centimeter. The customary standards would be cubic inches, and so on.	Ability to make estimates of volume in nonstandard units; measurements using cubes
136. Computing volume	4	5	6	The volume of an object considers three dimensions: its length, width, and depth. Area is the multiple of length and width (the square units on a surface), but volume is cubic units, and so we have to multiply by the depth as well.	As above using standard units; metric and useful customary such as cubic yard of firewood (see Geometry for more complex computations)
Money					
137. Vocabulary of coins, bills; American money; Foreign money; examples/ dollar value	K 6	K 7	1 8	Different coins represent different amounts of money. Different countries use different money standards; connect to exchange values and new Euro.	Correct identification; explanation of exchange value
138. Estimating and counting (in line with number sequence)	1	2	3	Each dime counts as ten pennies, each nickel is five pennies, and so on (Grade 1); quarters and halves (Grade 2).	Ability to total real and pictured coins
139. Place value connections: (a) whole dollars; (b) dollars and cents	1-2 2-3	2-3 3-4	4 5-6	Dollars come in units and multiples like our number system. See decimals for place value connections. Cents are parts of dollars. One hundred cents = 1 dollar.	Ability to rename dollar multiples from word problems

*NOTE: A = Exploration B = Concept Mastery C = Algorithmic or Procedural Mastery

CONTENT AREA BRANCHES	GRADE-LEVEL EXPECTATIONS*			CONTENT STANDARDS— Students Will Know That:	PERFORMANCE STANDARDS— Students Will Demonstrate Their Knowledge By:
Major and Minor	A	B	C		
140. Making change	1	2-3	4	We make change by counting up from cost to given quantity or down (whichever is easier); pennies or nickels to nearest dime (grade 1); pennies and/or nickels and/or dimes to nearest quarter, to nearest dollar (grade 2+). There is more than one way to give exact change.	Ability to estimate change; ability to give change by counting up or down without subtraction algorithm
141. Operations— adding/ subtracting	1	2-3	4	Money can be added or subtracted most easily by renaming or trading to the same coin or bill, or to pennies (hundredths of a dollar). Use real money, fake money, and calculators.	Ability to estimate totals, form properly placed algorithms from money word problems, and solve them with and without calculators
Time (Language check: rotary, digital, a.m., p.m.)					
142. Comparative time only, telling time	K	K	2	Words such as "longer," "less," "more," and "as much as" can be used to compare time. Hours and minutes are amounts of time. Clocks help us keep track of time in hours and minutes. They move with time! Larger amounts of time are days, weeks, months, and years.	Ability to recognize whole hours on the rotary clock and the digital clock; ability to relate specific times such as morning, noon, afternoon, and evening to activities and absence or presence of daylight
143. Telling time: whole hour	1	1	2	There are 24 whole hours in the day, 12 before and 12 after noon. The digital clock shows us the hour first and then minutes. The rotary clock shows us each whole passed hour by pointing to the number with its smaller hand. The larger hand shows minutes. See Chapter 3 for details.	Ability to tell whole-hour time from digital and rotary clocks
144. Telling time: Beginning, end, noon; a.m./p.m.	2	3	4	The day begins at midnight. It is divided into 24 hour parts: 12 before noon (a.m.) and 12 after noon (p.m.). Noon is when the sun is highest in the sky (or at the meridian). Morning is before noon, and afternoon is after it (a.m. stands for ante meridian, and p.m. stands for post meridian).	Ability to estimate and describe comparative amounts of elapsed time; ability to relate specific hours (e.g., 9:00 a.m.) to the position of the sun and the terms morning, afternoon, midnight, and noon

*NOTE: A = Exploration B = Concept Mastery C = Algorithmic or Procedural Mastery

CONTENT AREA BRANCHES	GRADE-LEVEL EXPECTATIONS*			CONTENT STANDARDS— Students Will Know That:	PERFORMANCE STANDARDS— Students Will Demonstrate Their Knowledge By:
Major and Minor	A	B	C		
145. Telling time: half hours quarters minutes	1 1 2	1 2 2	1 2 2	Each whole hour can be divided into two parts (halves or ½), four quarter parts (¼ hour), or 60 minute parts. There are four quarter hours in a whole hour and 60 minutes or minute parts in a whole hour. Half an hour is the same as 2 quarters, or 30 minutes (half of 60 minutes). We tell the time by naming the hour and the fractional part after it in halves or quarters or in the minutes after it.	Ability to explain the rotary clock in terms of its fractional parts; ability to rename half hours and quarter hours as minutes; ability to read digital and rotary clock time to the exact minute
146. Calculating elapsed time in hours, but not passing 12	2	3	4	When the clock has moved from 1 to 3, there is a difference of 2 hours; it is 2 hours later.	Ability to calculate elapsed time and solve word problems
147. Calculating elapsed time in hours, passing 12	3	4	5	To find the elapsed time passing 12, you must find two differences—before the 12 and after it—then add them together. When the clock has moved from 11 to 3, there is a difference of 4 hours—1 hour until noon and 3 hours from noon to 3.	Ability to solve and pose problems that require calculation of elapsed time from clock diagrams, and then from digital readings
148. Calculating elapsed time in minutes	2	3	4	To calculate the difference when you pass the hour, you must find two differences, before the hour and after it, then add them together.	As above, but passing the hour; then passing 12
149. Calendar: days in the week in sequence, months	K	1	2	There are 7 days in a week. There are 12 months in a year. There are 365 days in most years. Calendars help us keep track of larger amounts of time.	Ability to recall number and name of days of the week and months of the year; identify present, previous, and next day of week (and month); connect to events
150. Calendar: time of the year	1	1	2	Days of the month and year are shown on a calendar that also shows the weeks. Different days are related to different activities.	Ability to identify day, month, and year on calendar; recall months and connect to seasons, other events

*NOTE: A = Exploration   B = Concept Mastery   C = Algorithmic or Procedural Mastery

CONTENT AREA BRANCHES		GRADE-LEVEL EXPECTATIONS*			CONTENT STANDARDS— Students Will Know That:	PERFORMANCE STANDARDS— Students Will Demonstrate Their Knowledge By:
Major and Minor		A	B	C		
151.	Variations in calendar; days of month, year	2	3-4	5	Different months have different numbers of days. Each year, the days of the year may happen on different days of the week. Leap year has one more day for the year.	Ability to recall number of days in each month
152.	Calculating elapsed time in weeks, months	3	4	5	One week from Thursday is the following Thursday. If the 23rd is on Thursday, then the 30th is on Thursday.	Ability to identify 1 week before and after on the calendar; ability to predict day of the week given two dates 7 days apart—but only in the same month
153.	Determining days and dates of the week	3	4	5	Monday is 2 days before Wednesday and 3 days after Friday, and so on (let them use their fingers if they wish).	Ability to mentally calculate day of week given two dates up to 7 days apart and one day of the week (e.g., If the 23rd is on Tuesday, on what day is the 26th? If the 26th was on Friday, what day of the week was the 23rd?)
Temperature *(Language check: degree, temperature, thermometer, Fahrenheit, Celsius)*						
154.	Comparative temperature only	K	1	2	Temperature tells us how warm or cold something is.	Ability to compare perceived or felt temperature to room temperature
155.	Fahrenheit reading	2	3	4	A standard unit of measure for temperature is the degree. The warmer it is, the higher the temperature. Water freezes at 32°F(0°C) and boils at 212°F (100°C). Room temperature is about 70°F (25°C).	Ability to read and record temperature from a thermometer to the nearest degree; estimate colder or warmer than room temperature from reading; compute changes
	Celsius reading (whole degree)	3	4	5		

*NOTE: A = Exploration B = Concept Mastery C = Algorithmic or Procedural Mastery

CONTENT AREA BRANCHES	GRADE-LEVEL EXPECTATIONS*			CONTENT STANDARDS— Students Will Know That:	PERFORMANCE STANDARDS— Students Will Demonstrate Their Knowledge By:
Major and Minor	A	B	C		

Geometry: Visualizing shapes and patterns, models

(Language check: horizontal, vertical, perpendicular, polygon [and derivatives such as hexagon], symmetry, bilateral, radial, transform, flip, rotation, slide, congruent, similar plane, angle, vertex, circumference, radius, diameter.)

		A	B	C	CONTENT STANDARDS	PERFORMANCE STANDARDS
156.	Comparing and naming two-dimensional shapes (areas on a surface): Square, circle Triangle; Rectangle; Pentagon, hexagon; Quadrilateral	K 1 3 4 5	K 2 4 5 6	1 3 5 6 7	Shapes or forms on flat surfaces such as paper have different properties. Most of the shapes have sides and corners, but the circle and oval do not have any corners and only one side. Different shapes have different numbers of sides and corners and form different patterns. There are many different shapes and combinations of shapes in the environment. The names of shapes are derived from their properties. Familiar structures are named after their shapes (e.g., the Pentagon, a traffic circle).	Ability to identify shapes on paper and in the environment, at appropriate level; ability to count sides and corners, find patterns, reproduce shapes; ability to explain prefix-suffix meanings, polygon, hexagon Ability to construct shapes with computer
157.	Comparing shapes; relationship of perimeter and area to shape	6	7	8	The circle and the square have larger areas for a given perimeter than does the rectangle. Larger squares and circles have more area for a given perimeter than do smaller ones. The area increases at a faster rate than does the perimeter (use a data table to analyze).	Ability to solve problems that require computation of perimeters and areas (see measurement); ability to analyze relationship between perimeter and area and prove it
158.	Patterns congruent similar	K 3 5	1 4 6	2 5 7	Repeating the same shapes creates a pattern. Exact shapes, even in different positions, are congruent. Similar shapes may be different sizes, but have the same angles.	Constructing and identifying repeat unit in a pattern Constructing congruent and similar shapes
159.	Naming and comparing shapes of solid forms (3-D objects) that take up space	1	2	3	Solid forms are three-dimensional (3-D) objects that take up space. Solid forms have faces, edges, and corners. Different forms have different numbers of sides (edges), faces, and corners. The size of the edges of a solid form may be the same as or different from each other. There are patterns between the number of faces and the number of corners.	Identifying solid forms: cube, cylinder, sphere, prism, cone; counting faces, edges, corners; comparing shapes; finding patterns

---

*NOTE: A = Exploration B = Concept Mastery C = Algorithmic or Procedural Mastery

CONTENT AREA BRANCHES		GRADE-LEVEL EXPECTATIONS*			CONTENT STANDARDS— Students Will Know That:	PERFORMANCE STANDARDS— Students Will Demonstrate Their Knowledge By:
Major and Minor		A	B	C		
160.	Bilateral (mirror) symmetry	1-2	3	4	The same pattern in reverse on either side of a line creates mirror symmetry (use a MIRA here). Mirror symmetry can be created by reflecting across an imaginary line. We can find these patterns in the environment.	Identification of mirror symmetry; identification of mirror symmetry with a string and in environment Proof with MIRA
161.	Drawing symmetrical shapes and relating them to design	1-2	3	4-5	Patterns with mirror symmetry can be created with a flip from right to left across a line or from top to bottom (use drawings and software applications for practice).	Creation of patterns with mirror symmetry; connecting symmetry to design elements in art projects
162.	Radial symmetry	3	4	5	If you can rotate a form in any way and it is still the same, it has radial symmetry.	Identification of radial symmetry; construction of forms with radial symmetry
163.	Transformations	5	6	7	When you flip or rotate a figure or move it to the side (slip it), it has been transformed in its position on a plane, but the original figure and the one you transformed have the same dimensions and attributes, and we say they are congruent. Use computer software for this.	Ability to draw transformed figures and identify congruent triangles and parallelograms, solve problems that require reference to congruent objects; proof of congruence using computer-based transformations or cutouts
164.	Symmetry in number tables— triangular and square numbers	4	5	6	Number tables or objects can be constructed with symmetry and/or in shapes (e.g., triangular numbers 3, 6, 9 or square numbers 1, 4, 9, 16, 25).	Ability to recognize symmetry in a table, or to construct an object triangle from triangular numbers
165.	Definitions: point, line, horizontal, vertical, perpendicular	4	5	6	A point is a particular location in space. A line is a set of points. Horizontal lines are like the horizon: They go from left to right or right to left. Vertical lines go up and down from the horizon. When lines form a right angle with each other, we say the lines are perpendicular. A straight line goes infinitely in only two opposite (mirror image) directions and can be determined by any two points.	Ability to define and construct horizontal, vertical, and perpendicular lines; ability to identify them in the environment and connect them to architecture

---

*NOTE: A = Exploration B = Concept Mastery C = Algorithmic or Procedural Mastery

CONTENT AREA BRANCHES		GRADE-LEVEL EXPECTATIONS*			CONTENT STANDARDS— Students Will Know That:	PERFORMANCE STANDARDS— Students Will Demonstrate Their Knowledge By:
Major and Minor		A	B	C		
166.	Line segment, ray	5	6	7	A line segment is part of a line between two particular points. It includes all of the points in between the two particular ones. A ray is the part of the line that is going in one direction from one point on the line.	Ability to define and construct line segments and rays
167.	Definitions: planes	5	6	7	A plane is a surface determined by three points on that surface that are not on the same straight line. A line between any two points on the determined plane will be on that surface. A table top is often thought of as a plane surface, but the plane on which it is goes on infinitely. The legs of the table are on different planes.	Ability to determine whether a surface is a single plane; identification of different planes in three dimensional objects
168.	Parallel lines; parallelogram	5	6	7	Parallel lines are two separate lines that go in the same direction in the same plane and never cross. The parallelogram has opposite sides that are parallel.	Construction and identification of parallel lines, parallelograms
169.	Definitions: angles.	3	4	5	When two lines (rays) come from one endpoint, they form an angle. The point where they meet is called the vertex. The larger the opening between the lines, the larger the angle. Larger angles have a greater difference between the direction of their lines from their endpoint.	Ability to demonstrate and explain variations in angle size and relate them to differences in direction from an endpoint; ability to draw and compare smaller and larger angles using a straightedge
170.	Measuring circles and angles	5	6	7	Measures of angles and circles are related because if you keep increasing the size of an angle by rotating one ray until you are back to where you started, you have rotated all the way around, and every point on the ray has described a circle. The standard is to divide the circle into 360 degree units and a symbol (°) is used. A half circle (semicircle) is 180°. A quarter circle is 90°.	Making connections between angles and circles by demonstrating drawing and explaining; identifying degrees in full circle, semicircle, quarter circle; connecting circles to symmetry and making transformations of semicircles

*NOTE: A = Exploration B = Concept Mastery C = Algorithmic or Procedural Mastery

CONTENT AREA BRANCHES		GRADE-LEVEL EXPECTATIONS*			CONTENT STANDARDS— Students Will Know That:	PERFORMANCE STANDARDS— Students Will Demonstrate Their Knowledge By:
Major and Minor		A	B	C		
171.	Measuring angles	5	6	7	We measure angles or the opening between the rays in degrees. The higher the number of degrees, the greater the difference between the lines (rays). The measure of an angle is the same as the part of the circle it has described. If you rotate a ray halfway around to form a semicircle, the ray has formed a straight line or straight angle of 180°. The total distance rotated is 180° degrees.	Demonstration of angle formation by physical rotation of two straight edges; comparing relative size of angles
172.	Special angles; measuring angles with protractors	5	6	7	A straight line is also a straight angle of 180° that has two rays coming from one point in opposite directions. If we rotate one ray from the straight angle halfway to 180°, the two rays are perpendicular and form a 90° angle. The 90° angle is also called a right angle.	Using a protractor to draw exact angles; ability to measure angles with a protractor; identifying right angles; making right-angle transformations
173.	Using compasses to construct circles	3	4	5	The compass allows you to draw a set of points all equally distant from the center. This is a circle. The protractor allows you to draw specific angles. Exploration only of relative size of circles at this level.	Using the compass to draw a circle and the line to the center point; ability to predict relative size of the edge of a circle when comparing measured lines to the center point
174.	Measuring circles; value of pi	5 6	6 7	7 8	The distance around the edge of the circle is called the circumference. The distance from the center to the edge is the radius, and the distance from one point on the edge through the center to the opposite edge is the diameter. The length of the diameter is always twice the length of the radius. The circumference of a circle is always a certain number of times larger than the diameter. It is a constant value represented by a Greek letter called pi (π). We can compute pi by measuring the diameters and circumferences of several circles.	Ability to describe and compare circles using the terms diameter, radius, and circumference; ability to predict relative size of circumference from given diameters; ability to estimate and then compute circumference from diameter (see Chapter 3 for activities that construct the meaning and value of pi)

*NOTE: A = Exploration B = Concept Mastery C = Algorithmic or Procedural Mastery

CONTENT AREA BRANCHES	GRADE-LEVEL EXPECTATIONS*			CONTENT STANDARDS—Students Will Know That:	PERFORMANCE STANDARDS—Students Will Demonstrate Their Knowledge By:
Major and Minor	A	B	C		
175. Surface area of three-dimensional figures	6	7	8	The surface area of three-dimensional figures is the sum of the areas of all planes. Different figures have different relationships of volume to surface area.	Analyzing and comparing relative size of surface areas for three-dimensional objects (e.g., cube vs. flat cylinder, sphere vs. cone); ability to compute surface area of cube and cylinder

Data/tables/graphs: Models/multiple representation/algebra functions
(Language check: data, attributes, interval, reference line)

CONTENT AREA BRANCHES	A	B	C	CONTENT STANDARDS	PERFORMANCE STANDARDS
176. Data-gathering organization; tallying	1	2	3	Data must be recorded and organized to have meaning for others. Data can be collected and tallied or added up.	Ability to organize loose data; ability to use tallies and interpret them
177. Analysis: Comparison of data	2	3	4	Data can be compared when it is organized. Data gathering is subject to error.	Ability to analyze data and predict errors in gathering
178. Data tables	2	3-4	5-6	A data table helps us organize measured attributes or events. It helps us see patterns more clearly and plan for other models.	Ability to analyze and construct data tables with appropriate labels and intervals; recognize patterns from tables
179. Simple pictographs	K	1	2	A graph is a picture or model of measured quantities or data. The pictures help us see values clearly and compare them. We need a key and labels to tell us what the pictures mean. It is useful to use equally measured spaces or intervals on graphs.	Ability to record data, construct, and interpret simple pictographs (with verbalized explanations)
180. Bar graphs (construction/interpretation)	1	2	3	Another graph is the bar graph. Two perpendicular lines are used as starting places or reference lines. We label the reference lines to tell what they represent. The distance from one reference line to the end of the bar shows the data value; the other line separates the categories. Bar graphs show differences well.	Ability to analyze and compare quantities from bar graphs; ability to construct bar graphs on paper and on computer from data tables; ability to justify choice of bar graph

*NOTE: A = Exploration B = Concept Mastery C = Algorithmic or Procedural Mastery

CONTENT AREA BRANCHES	GRADE-LEVEL EXPECTATIONS*			CONTENT STANDARDS— Students Will Know That:	PERFORMANCE STANDARDS— Students Will Demonstrate Their Knowledge By:
Major and Minor	A	B	C		
181. Simple line graphs, tree and stem graphs	4	5	6	Line graphs can be used to show how often particular measures occur. They give you a good idea about how data are distributed. The tree and stem graph is similar and an efficient way to use graphs.	Extracting data from a line graph; identifying areas where greatest number of events occurred; construction of a line graph from data table
182. Time lines (construction/ interpretation)	4	5	6	Events can be recorded on lines in order of their occurrence either from left to right or bottom to top. Distance between events should relate to the time between their occurrences.	Ability to interpret event sequence from a time line; ability to construct a time line from a story and/or real-life adventure
183. Circle (pie) graphs; relative size of parts Estimation of part to whole	3 4	4 5	5 6	A pie graph shows differences between different elements of a data set, but it also shows how one part is related to the whole. For example, it can show how many students in a class got between 90 and 100 on a test and compare that to how many got between 50 and 60; it can then show what part the 90-100 group is of the whole class. The circle represents the whole data set, and the pie pieces represent the size of each part.	Ability to analyze pie graphs and compare relative (more or less than) quantities of elements pictured in a pie graph; ability to estimate size of one element as fractional part of whole
184. Pie graph; computation of exact size of part from angle measure	6	7	8	The size of a piece of a pie graph is the measure of the central angle it describes. If a whole circle is 360°, then an angle of 90° is $\frac{1}{4}$ of the whole circle.	Ability to construct a simple pie graph from data and use computers for more difficult angles
185. Choosing appropriate representations	6	7	8	Different graphs and representations are used to show data. The choice depends on the ideas you wish to communicate.	Ability to explain and justify choice of a graph; ability to connect use of different graphs to different sets of data

*NOTE: A = Exploration B = Concept Mastery C = Algorithmic or Procedural Mastery

CONTENT AREA BRANCHES		GRADE-LEVEL EXPECTATIONS*			CONTENT STANDARDS— Students Will Know That:	PERFORMANCE STANDARDS— Students Will Demonstrate Their Knowledge By:
Major and Minor		A	B	C		
186.	Using coordinates to locate positions on a grid and follow directions with a map	3	4	5	Coordinates are equally measured spaces, like those on a map, that can help us show and find things. You need two perpendicular reference lines coming from one point or origin for your grid. Two measured distances on the lines from the origin locate a specific point on a plane. We usually show the value of the measured distances as ordered pairs of values, and show distance on the horizontal line first.	Ability to locate points on a grid from an ordered pair of distances from a line (Have each child put a dot on a blank piece of paper and try to describe where it is; then do with geoboard or grid paper. This is a good language arts skill as well as social studies articulation point.)
187.	Using coordinates to show relationships between variables; writing equations	6	7	8	Coordinates like those on a grid show the relationship between variable values. If we see a pattern for the relationship between variables, we can write an algebraic equation that shows the relationship. See Chapter 3 for exemplars.	Ability to recognize and analyze relationships; write algebraic equations (functions) to express them
188.	Line graphs using coordinates	6	7	8	Line graphs using coordinate points are useful for showing how two variables are related or how a variable changes over time. We call the horizontal reference line the x-axis and the vertical reference line the y-axis. We connect the coordinates that show the related points with lines. If there is a consistent pattern in the relationship between the values of two variables, that relationship can be described as a mathematical function.	Ability to translate data tables showing two related variables into coordinates and line graphs; ability to describe unchanging relationships as a mathematical function (e.g., the increase in the side of a square and its area: $A = s^2$)
189.	Rate of change, slope	6	7	8	If one variable changes quickly in relation to the other, the slope of the line will be steep. Steep slopes form larger angles with reference lines. A steep hill takes you up faster than does a gradual hill.	Ability to predict slope of line graph from a two-variable data table; express comparative rate of change in two sets of two variables (e.g., altitude reached compared to distance traveled on a steep and gradual hill)

___

*NOTE: A = Exploration B = Concept Mastery C = Algorithmic or Procedural Mastery

CONTENT AREA BRANCHES	GRADE-LEVEL EXPECTATIONS*			CONTENT STANDARDS— Students Will Know That:	PERFORMANCE STANDARDS— Students Will Demonstrate Their Knowledge By:
Major and Minor	A	B	C		
190. Possible extension to negative quadrants	4	5	6	It is sometimes necessary to locate points on the other side of the two reference lines of a graph. A good example would be below-zero weather on a very cold day.	Ability to predict the necessity of locating points on the other side of the two reference lines
Probability and statistics: Models/multiple representation/functions					
191. Chance events, certainty/ uncertainty	K	1	2	Sometimes, things are certain to occur, and other times, there is only a chance that they will happen.	Ability to distinguish between certain and chance events
192. Equal or unequal outcome possibilities	3	3-4	4-5	Outcomes are not always equally expected. For example, there is a greater chance of a warm day in July than in March—although it could happen.	Ability to identify factors that affect outcome of chance events; ability to compute simple unequal outcome probabilities
193. Predicting outcomes	2	3	4	Sometimes, we can predict the probability of uncertain events. If there are two choices on the spinner, we can predict that each choice will come up half of the time. If there are more choices on the spinner, each choice will happen fewer times. If one die has only numbers 1, 2, and 3 on it, and the other die has 1, 2, 3, 4, 5, and 6, which one will show number 2 the most?	Ability to compare probability of individual events given the number of choices; construction of a tree diagram or table of probable events
194. Proof of inferences	3	4	5	We can prove our predictions by collecting data, but the data will not always be exact. The more data we collect, the closer we get to our prediction.	Proof of inference by collecting and collating data

---

*NOTE: A = Exploration B = Concept Mastery C = Algorithmic or Procedural Mastery

CONTENT AREA BRANCHES		GRADE-LEVEL EXPECTATIONS*			CONTENT STANDARDS— Students Will Know That:	PERFORMANCE STANDARDS— Students Will Demonstrate Their Knowledge By:
Major and Minor		A	B	C		
195.	Combinations: order independent	2	3-4	4	Different objects can be combined into different groups or sets, but a given number of objects can be combined in only a certain number of ways. Tree diagrams and tables record combinations. You can make six different combinations of two objects out of four different objects if the way or order of how the objects are combined doesn't matter (e.g., for objects R, W, Y, and B; there can be RW, WY, YB, RB, WB, and RY.	Ability to explain that objects can be arranged differently; ability to compute number of sets of two from three or four different objects using real objects and tables. Ability to construct a tree diagram or table of possible events
196.	Combinations: order-dependent two objects combined	4	5	6	Sometimes, the order does matter. Then, there are more possibilities because a switched order of the two objects makes a different case.	Proof of inference using tree diagrams as real data
197.	Permutations: more than two objects	6	7	8	As the number of objects combined into one group increases, the number of possibilities changes. If the order doesn't matter, a tree diagram will show that there are only four possibilities for four objects grouped into threes, and only one for four objects grouped into four. If the order does matter, four objects can be grouped into groups of three 24 different ways. (A good problem here is to consider how many times four teams in a league can play each other without repeating regardless of where they play, and then determine how many different games they can play with each other if a home game is different from an away game.)	Construction of a tree diagram or table of possible events; generalizations about the relationships between number of objects in a group and possibilities
198.	Central tendency: finding the average or mean	5	6	7	The average (mean) of several measured quantities helps you interpret the data. An average makes it easier to consider the whole group or data set rather than many different, separate measures. We find the mean by adding up all of the separate quantities in a set of data and dividing by the number of quantities. Values that are very different from most values are called outliers, and sometimes, they are omitted from the mean because they affect the mean too much and may be incorrect data.	Ability to estimate and compute means and explain them; explanation of how outliers affect mean (Batting averages are also ratios. They tell us what proportion of the times at bat resulted in hits. The total number of hits for the player is divided by the number of times at bat. Why is a batting average usually less than 1? What other kinds of data could give us an average less than 1?)

*NOTE: A = Exploration B = Concept Mastery C = Algorithmic or Procedural Mastery

CONTENT AREA BRANCHES		GRADE-LEVEL EXPECTATIONS*			CONTENT STANDARDS— Students Will Know That:	PERFORMANCE STANDARDS— Students Will Demonstrate Their Knowledge By:
Major and Minor		A	B	C		
199.	The median	6	7	8	Medians also tell us something about the whole group. The median is the value in the middle. You find the median by lining up all the data in order, counting the number of entries and then finding the middle score, which has an equal number of scores above and below. If the number of scores is even, then you have to find the average of the two middle scores. Medians and means are sometimes close but not the same. Outliers do not make a difference in medians.	Computation of median and explanations of the value
200.	Graphing distributions: line graphs and box-and-whiskers graphs	6	7	8	Sometimes, it is also useful to see how all scores, or one in particular, are distributed around the mean or median. Line graphs and box-and-whiskers graphs can be used to show the distribution of individual scores and the median or mean or both.	Construction of line and box-and-whiskers graphs that show distribution; analysis of box-and-whiskers graphs to evaluate data and collection methods

*NOTE: A = Exploration B = Concept Mastery C = Algorithmic or Procedural Mastery

CHAPTER 3

Scaffolds for Teachers and Problems for Students

A Guide to Chapter 3

Chapter 3 is designed as a supplement to Chapter 2. It provides some of the instructional ideas for achieving the concepts listed by number in Chapter 2. These ideas are based on the work of many mathematics education researchers (some of whom are listed in the references), my own observations of children and preservice teachers as they learned, and the observations of the experienced teachers with whom I work. The numbers in Chapter 3 correspond to the numbers in Chapter 2. In some cases, they have been consolidated into groups to encourage teachers to backtrack to the foundation concepts.

The illustrative examples are almost entirely original and somewhat different from textbook problems in their presentation. They may take students over several development levels and connect to other concepts. They are meant to be used as an interactive support in the scaffolding process as the teacher guides students in the construction of new knowledge. Teachers may wish to copy the exemplars for use with their students, but they may need to adapt some of them to the developmental level of their students. Many of the exemplars involve group activities.

They represent only a limited sample of the kind of challenges that teachers will need in order to help students develop a wide range of problem-solving skills. Teachers should consult the many additional scaffolding ideas and sample problems in the NCTM (1989, 2000) standards documents and other sources listed in the references. Mathematics textbooks meant for use by children also have many problems and activities that can be used along with these examples for further practice and challenges.

The algorithms for which scaffolding is suggested are, for the most part, the standard algorithms. Technology makes most algorithms less important, but they are fast, accurate, and powerful, and they provide a written record (Usikin,

1998). We need to recognize that different algorithms are standards in other places or have been the standard form at different times.

Learned with meaning, algorithms may also help students understand mathematical relationships and patterns. Concurrently, students should be encouraged to try to develop their own algorithms and perhaps share them with others. The value of student-invented algorithms is that the process of invention firmly constructs mathematical concepts. This value is further enhanced by opportunities to describe the invented procedure. Even if the invention is not as efficient as the standard procedure, it should be recognized as valid. Student attention, however, should be called to the relative efficiency of standard algorithms. In any case, teachers should avoid spending too much time on drill and practice with algorithms—there are too many other useful mathematics ideas that students have to learn.

Most of the concrete manipulatives suggested are among those in most common use, available from educational supply companies, and there are many additional forms that are useful. Some of the other manipulative suggestions, such as the shoe-box roll with pom-poms and egg carton fractions, may not be as familiar to teachers. However, they are easily constructed.

The suggested technology applications are just the tip of the iceberg. Many of the new generation software applications can be used as supplements to help provide additional experiences. Using common drawing applications students can construct their own chips and duplicate and manipulate them. They can create figures, rotate them, and transform them. They can use interactive probes to collect original data on temperature or light, organize the data into tables, plot graphs, and perform operations with handheld calculators. Over the Internet, students can retrieve data such as seismographic readings, temperature, distances, and annual rainfall from all over the world.

The overriding concept, however, is that we all learn by *doing* mathematics.

1 Counting begins as a rote repetition of the number words, but learners soon develop concepts of quantity, such as more, less, many, few, and *a whole bunch*. They then begin to understand the sequence as an increasing number line. One-to-one correspondence is the understanding that each item counted has a different number word in the counting sequence and represents a different position on the number line. Pointing to or touching the item as it is counted is both good practice and an indicator of concept construction. Use real things and manipulatives such as beads and chips, as well as pictures. To help develop the concept of increasing quantity, ask in reference to the figure: *"One more horse would be how many, and one more than that would be . . .?"*

Count the horses; touch each one and say the number name.

Touch the horse with the number name 2.

Touch the number 4 horse.

Put a circle around the numbers 2 and 4 on the number line.

1   2   3   4   5   6

Count the balls. Count the jacks.

Count them on the number line.

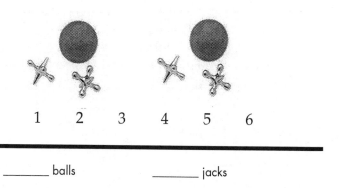

1   2   3   4   5   6

_____ balls   _____ jacks

*** Make your own bead frames. Bead frames are great because they stay in place. Each child should have one in his or her desk. Use a 10- by 12-inch piece of pegboard and plastic cord to string 10 beads at a time. Let the children make them. I like using one color bead for several conceptual reasons. You can also make a bead frame for the overhead projector by drilling holes in a sheet of clear, hard plastic and stringing it.

Manipulatives are analogies for the real things. You can help students make the analogy transition to the manipulatives by asking questions such as: "What does each bead mean?" or "What does each bead stand for?"

2 Some children will not attain *cardinal principle* or the concept that the last number counted represents the size of the group, until the second or third grade. Not having the concept will delay their ability to add and subtract with meaning. Teachers will note that children without the concept always recount each item when adding. They can see addition as an increase in the number line, but do not start from the last number counted.

Try using two-sided chips, turning each as it is counted.

Cover up a just-counted group and ask: "How many did you count?" Keep extending the wait time before asking the question. Or have the children count items in their hands and then put their hands behind their backs and ask the "how many" question. Counting without the number line and in various arrangements will also help.

3 Practice in counting objects spaced differently and in different arrangements should help the *conservation* of number concept develop.

This concept may also be strengthened by simultaneously providing opportunities for students to pour liquids into different containers and asking them if the amount of liquid changed.

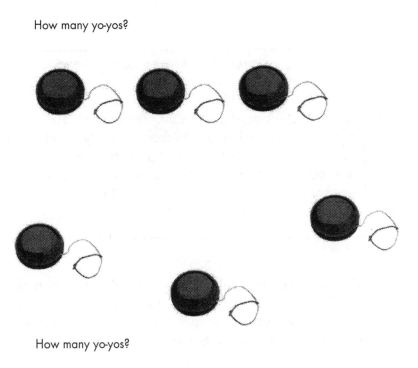

How many yo-yos?

How many yo-yos?

4 *Sorting* and *seriation* are related, and both require the ability to distinguish between the name of the object and its properties. Seriation seems to be more intrinsically related to natural development of magnitude. Strong seriation and sorting concepts will help with more complex kinds of attribute and pattern recognition. Use size and other attributes to help students develop this concept as they put real objects in order of the changing amount of a single property, and always ask for identification of the property.

Some critical scaffolding questions for seriation are:

Here are some helmets. What is the same about them? What is different? They are all football helmets, but they are different sizes. Can we arrange them to show the differences in size order?

Here are some eight balls. How are they the same? How are they different? Can we put them in order of how dark they are? Is there any other order we can use?

**Let the children learn to use a computer drawing program to change the size of the repeated object, and then have them put their objects in order.

Number all the helmets according to size. Number the smallest helmet (1) and the largest helmet (3).

Do you see any other differences?

Number all the 8 balls according to how large they are. Number the smallest (1) and the largest (3). Do you see any other differences? Can you number them differently for other properties?

5 The critical scaffolding questions for *sorting* are as follows:

What makes these the same? What makes them different?

For distinguishing between an object and its properties, the critical questions are the following:

Can you think of another object with a different name that has the same property? What property makes them the same? Put all of the things that have that property together in a group. Why are some things not in the group? Are there other ways to sort these same items?

There are many commercial sorting materials available, but you can use common items such as beans, toys, and foods. Make connections to language arts by sorting words according to their properties, and then stories according to their common themes. Make connections to social studies by grouping cities, states, and countries. Make connections to science by sorting living and nonliving things.

6 Beyond rote repetition of the number names, the teen numbers are sometimes difficult conceptual hurdles for students. Use a bead frame to build the concept of 10 and one more, two more, three more, and so on. Popsicle sticks that children can tie into groups of 10 with rubber bands are useful here. Ten frames and counting tables are also helpful.

Number all the animals from (1) to (3). Number the slowest runner (1) and the fastest runner (3). How are the animals the same? How are they different?

What properties make them the same? What properties make them different? Which two are the most alike? Why?

_____   _____   _____

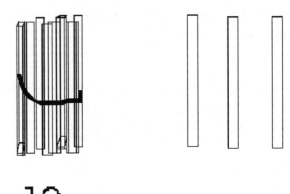

10

How many popsicle sticks?

  Solomon, P. *The Math We Need to "Know" and "Do": Content Standards for Elementary and Middle Grades.* © 2001. Corwin Press, Inc.

7   Being able to visually recognize the size of a small group without counting each item (subitize) is a useful skill. Let the children come up with their own schemes for doing this, but encourage them to verbalize and share them.

Look quickly at the happy faces. Try not to count them one by one. *How many are there? Explain how you knew that.*

8 & 12   Counting by 10 and an introduction to place value should come together. "Base 10" blocks, stacked unifix cubes, packages of Popsicle™ sticks, and other groups of materials (money also can be used) should be used simultaneously with a number table up to 100.

The critical transition is from the rote repetition of the decades to the understanding that 10 is added each time. Adding 10 with a calculator is also helpful.

How did we get from 10 to 20, from 20 to 30?
Give me 20.
Give me 10 more.
How many did you give me?

Count the blocks by ten. Find the total on the number table. How many tens did you count? How many ones?

1	2	3	4	5	6	7	8	9	10
11	12	13	14	15	16	17	18	19	20
21	22	23	24	25	26	27	28	29	30
31	32	33	34	35	36	37	38	39	40
41	42	43	44	45	46	47	48	49	50
51	52	53	54	55	56	57	58	59	60
61	62	63	64	65	66	67	68	69	70
71	72	73	74	75	76	77	78	79	80
81	82	83	84	85	86	87	88	89	90
91	92	93	94	95	96	97	98	99	100

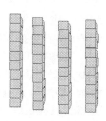

9   There are two phases for *skip counting*. The first phase is an understanding of skip counting as it relates rote repetition of counting tables to the number line. Do not completely discount the rote memorization of the counts. Rhythmic language patterns will help them develop. However, instead of just memorizing the counting tables, students can see the sequence as a pattern of skipping numbers on the number line. Begin with skip counting by two and its relationship to odd and even numbers.

Make the connection to sharing division. Line up a variety of manipulatives and divide them into two groups to allow students to discover why numbers are odd or even. Relate the mathematical terms to their common language usage.

Children can act out the skip counts by arranging themselves in a line and actually "skipping out" by two and three. Musical rhythms also can be useful. Children learn the concept that skip counting omits numbers on the line or emphasizes beats on the drum. Skip counting can also show doubling patterns. For example, counting by four skips a count by two, but the doubling concept may be developed more readily after the transition to multiple groups has been made.

We started at zero. How many boys did we skip before we got to three? How many from three to six? How do we get to nine?

Let's put the boys in groups. How many groups to get to six? How many in each group?

  Solomon, P. *The Math We Need to "Know" and "Do": Content Standards for Elementary and Middle Grades.* © 2001. Corwin Press, Inc.

9 The second phase for skip counting is a transition from the number line concept to multiplication as repeated addition or the idea that each time you skip to the next number, you add on a group of two, three, or four, and so on. Scaffolding questions for this transition include the following: *How did you skip count 0, 3, 6, 9, 12? How did you get from 6 to 9? How much more is 6 than 3, 9 than 6, 12 than 9? How many skips of three from 0 to 12? How many times did you add three? How much is four times three?* This is also a good place to introduce doubling patterns for multiplication. The bead frame and calculators can also be used to support the skip counting concept. *How much is four threes? How many times did you hit the key to add three? How much did it add up to? How much is five times three?*

10
10a Conceptual understanding of our algorithm for combining or adding negative and positive integers may also be helped by relating it to a number line with zero at the center. Positive values go toward the right of zero and negative values to the left. Movements in one direction cancel movements in the other direction.

Other demonstrations of the canceling concept may help in understanding what happens when integers are combined. Some of the tracking systems in the new video games can be used for motivation here. If you gain six lives and lose two, how many do you have left? If you win three dollars and lose two, how many do you have left? Both of these problems can be translated to the number line and demonstrated with two-sided chips to show positive and negative values. The result may easily be seen as positive or negative depending upon what you had more of. In a card game, a pulled diamond card takes away a spade. How many spades would you have left in your hand if you pulled six spades and four diamonds from the deck? ♠ ♠ ♠ ♠ ♠ ♠ + ♦ ♦ ♦ ♦ =

Count by four. Four, one time, is four. Four, two times, is eight. Four, three times, is 12. Three times four is _____.

Double the count. Four, six times, is _____. Six times four is _____.

If a pickup travels four miles in one direction from the starting place (zero) and then turns around and travels six miles in the opposite direction, where does it end up in relation to where it started?
($^+$4) + ($^-$6) =

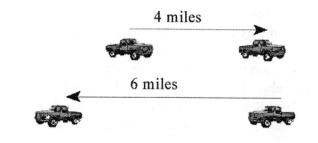

4 miles

6 miles

5 4 3 2 1 0 1 2 3 4 5

10b Demonstrations of the subtraction of integers on the number line are more difficult, but useful in understanding how they work. If we think of subtraction as finding the difference (see 31) or distance between any two values, that distance is an absolute value. On the number line, starting from the lowest value to find the difference always makes us move in a positive direction. In the common vertical subtraction algorithm, we usually place the higher value on top; if we count up from the lower positive value to the higher value, the difference is positive. When we subtract a negative value in the integer algorithm, a change in sign for the integer to the positive is necessary before combining (adding) the values to get the total distance or difference between them.

As an example, the difference between 3 degrees below zero and 4 degrees above is seven degrees. To find the difference, we add the degrees below zero to those above zero. The confusing thing in the algorithm is that we use the same sign to show both a negative value and the subtraction operation. We, therefore, show the negative value with a superscript to distinguish it from the operation sign. $4 - (^-3)$ becomes $4 + 3$ and equals 7. On the number line, to find the difference between two negative integers $(^-2)$ and $(^-6)$, we count up +4 from the lower $(^-6)$ value. In a combining integers algorithm, starting with the higher value, $(^-2) - (^-6)$ means the difference between them. It will equal $^+4$ only if we change the negative integer that is subtracted to a positive one and add.

We can then make the generalization that when we subtract a negative number, the negatives cancel each other and we add a positive value. This generalization that two negatives become a positive can also be reinforced with verbal logic. *"I do not not have the right time"* means that I have it.

Two pickup trucks left a rest stop at the same time. They traveled in opposite directions. One traveled six miles in one direction from the starting place, and the other traveled four miles in the opposite direction from the starting place. What is the distance between them?

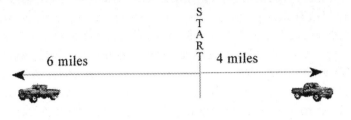

6 miles   S T A R T   4 miles

6 5 4 3 2 1 0 1 2 3 4 5

Finish the equation: $(^+4)-(^-6)=$ _____

The low temperature in Fairbanks, Alaska, was five degrees below zero on Monday and two degrees below zero on Saturday. How much warmer was it on Saturday? How do we count the difference on the number line?

6° 5° 4° 3° 2° 1° 0° 1° 2° 3° 4° 5°
Mon   Sat

This equation is the common way for finding the difference between the two temperatures:

$$(^-2)-(^-5)=\text{\_\_\_\_}$$

Why did we start with the Saturday temperature? How can we come up with the same answer as we did by counting on the number line?

A chip game gives you a red side when you answer a question correctly and a yellow side when you make a mistake. No chips are given for unanswered questions. The most red chips win, but yellow chips cancel red ones.

Yellow ○   Red ●

Fred ○ ○ ○   Alex ○ ○ ○ ○ ○
● ● ● ● ● ● ●   ● ● ● ● ● ● ●

Decide who is the loser in this game. How many extra right answers are needed by the loser to tie the game? Does it pay to guess answers?
Finish the equation: $(^+7)+(^-3)-(^+7)+(^-5)=$ _____
Why did we start with Fred?

11   Make the connection between the word *ordinal* and the fact that the order counts for ordinal numbers. Children grasp this concept easily—perhaps because it has so much application in sports, their games, and personal competition.

12   Place value concepts are very critical for understanding, but often are not completely developed. There are several conceptual transitions that must be made.

1.   The move from one-to-one correspondence to cardinal principle should be followed or accompanied quickly by the idea that we can think of groups or sets of individual items or values as a whole.

2.   The next step is combining sets that are the same and counting by 10 (see above): We counted three tens. How many do we have?

3.   A sometimes overlooked transition is the ability to *visualize one single item as a symbol for a group of 10 (or more)*. This is the concept of *one-to-many correspondence*.

4.   The next and important transition is understanding that the value of a symbol can *change with its position*.

Manipulatives can help with each transition. For the first two steps, any kind of grouped materials work well. Grid sheets and base 10 blocks can be introduced here, but be careful to make the analogy of the manipulative to the real thing. This is also a good time to make the money connections. One dime represents 10 pennies, and one dollar represents 100 pennies. One 10-dollar bill is the same as 10 singles. Card trading games are also applicable.

Evan said that the third person on the stage was his friend Fred. Jim said that Fred was the sixth person on the stage. Explain why they are both right. Can you tell how many people were on the stage?

Color in the tens grid to show the number of ones cubes.

_____ tens and _____ ones = _____

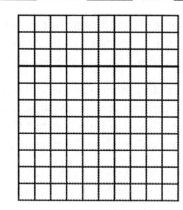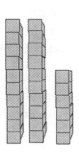

_____ hundred, _____ tens, and _____ ones = _____

_____ tens and _____ ones = _____

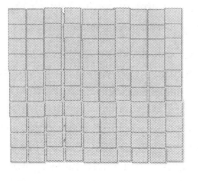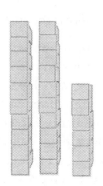

13 Base 10 blocks are also useful for one-to-many correspondence, but because you can still see the individual ones, I like to use different sizes of pom-poms for the transition to seeing a single symbol as representative of many. Pom-poms are excellent for the shoebox roll activities for place value and combinations because they are inexpensive, varied, soft, and quiet. However, you can also use large and small lima beans.

1. Begin by using large and small pom-poms, with the single large pom-pom a symbol for 10. Follow this with different colored pom-poms for ones and tens.

2. For the final transition to position as the value indicator, use the same color and size pom-poms because you want students to develop the idea that the same symbol in a different position has a different value.

3. Students can also construct their own images of the shoebox roll using draw programs on the computer.

4. Let students discover that using the same number of pom-poms can create different values, and larger numbers of pom-poms can show lesser values.

5. Let students discover why zero is needed as a place holder as they see an empty center box and try to express the quantity in number symbols.

Make a shoebox roll by dividing an ordinary empty shoebox into two sections with a piece of construction paper, and label the sections "ones" and "tens." Leave enough room on top of the partition for the pom-poms to roll over it. Cover the box and shake it to achieve various values. The children can work with individual boxes in pairs, and you can also use a clear plastic box on the overhead projector. Then divide the boxes into three sections, adding one for hundreds.

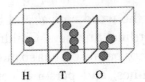
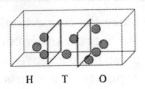

H   T   O   H   T   O

153 = 1 hundred + 5 tens + 3 ones | 324 = 3 hundreds + 2 tens + 4 ones

Nine pom-poms roll in the place value shoebox in different ways.
Show how nine pom-poms can add up to 234.
Could you add nine more pom-poms and only show a value of 99?

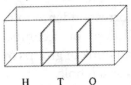
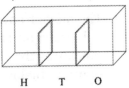

H   T   O   H   T   O

___ hundreds + ___ tens + ___ ones = 234 | ___ hundreds + ___ tens + ___ ones = 99

Can you use the same number of pom-poms to show 909?

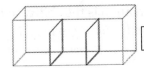

___ hundreds + ___ tens + ___ ones = 909

13 Practice with base 10 blocks and simultaneous notation of symbolic forms are useful as students develop the concept of a systematic one-to-many pattern of equalities in our number system. Trading games with the blocks and with money are supportive. Making these simultaneous with the renaming of the number symbol form for quantities in different ways will strengthen student ability to deal with complex computations and develop number sense. The number 1,232 is one thousand, 2 hundreds, 3 tens, and 2 ones, but it is also 12 hundreds, 3 tens, and 2 ones, and it is also 123 tens and 2 ones, or just 1,232 ones. Ask questions such as: *When are larger units necessary? When are smaller units needed?* Again, connections to money, baseball cards, or Pokémon™[1] trading games can be helpful as familiar analogies to the process.

14 The next place value transition is the shift from the concept of equality to the concept of multiple. One 10 is equal to 10 ones, but it is also 10 times larger. When asked, "How much larger is the 10 than the one?" children will correctly say that the 10 is nine more. The enlargement concept of multiplication as it is related to place value needs careful scaffolding. "How many times larger?" is better. Use the base 10 blocks to demonstrate this concept, carefully beginning with just the units and showing groups that are one time larger, two times larger, and three times larger before shifting to the 10.

Blowing up balloons is also effective here. Equal sizes of balloons have one time as much air as the original. Two times as much air is in a balloon twice as large. Use the balloons or drawings, or have students enlarge a diagram made with a computer-based drawing program. Make a copy and then enlarge the original several times. Write the number sentence for each enlargement.

Make even trades.
Trade the blocks below for: 12 hundreds and _____ tens and _____ ones.
Trade them for: one thousand, and _____ tens and 4 ones.
Trade them for: _____ ones.
Can you find another even trade?

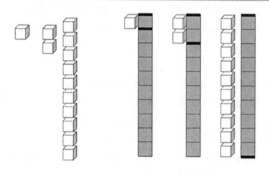

1 time, 2 times, 10 times as many ones.

1 time, 2 times, 10 times as much air.

14 Each unit in a place is 10 times larger than the same unit to its right. To make a unit 10 times larger, you shift it to the left; to make it 10 times smaller, you shift it to the right. Let the students play shift games, lining themselves up like the number symbols. Each student is given a unit value, and competing teams try different lineups to see which has the greatest total value. Be sure to use zero values and record symbols for different regroupings (e.g., 1 hundred, 2 tens, and 3 ones, or 12 tens and 3 ones, or 123 ones). Then, multiply the values by using a left shift as a bonus for quick arrangements of given quantities and division by right shift as a penalty for the slowest.

The shoebox roll is also excellent for this concept, and students should discover both the need for zero as a place holder and the effect of left and right shifts.

Move quickly to multiplication of number symbols by 10 and 100 and division by 10 and 100. The question of how to divide ones by 10 should lead to the concept of decimal fractions and the extension of the place value system to values less than one whole. How can we show values less than one whole? Why do we need a decimal point? Read the decimal point as "and," and the decimal values as the smallest place.

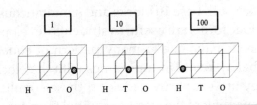

Fill in the right number symbol. Be sure to use zero as a placeholder.

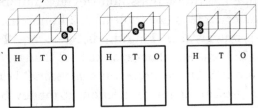

Make this value 10 times larger.

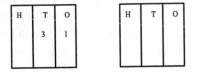

Make this value 10 times smaller.

Solomon, P. *The Math We Need to "Know" and "Do": Content Standards for Elementary and Middle Grades.* © 2001. Corwin Press, Inc.

15 Decimal place value concepts should follow review activities with whole numbers as above. The concept of decimal place values can be connected concurrently to the division application of fractions (partition form).

Shifting one place to the right makes a unit 10 times smaller. What fractional part of a whole is 10 times smaller than the whole? Dividing a number by 10 is like finding what fractional part of it? How can we find one tenth of a number by shifting places? And how can we find 10% of a number by shifting places?

Make this value 10 times smaller.

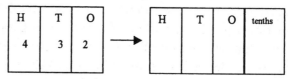

Make this value 10 times larger.

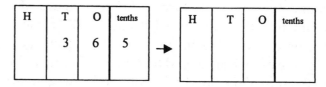

Find one tenth of this value.

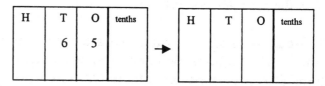

16 Conventional rounding is an important number sense
** skill, but it should be considered in the context of other
17 estimation approaches. Some of the difficulty students have had with the rounding convention for larger numbers may be the traditional focus just on the number 5 rather than on the concept that five tens are half of one hundred and five hundreds are half of one thousand. Scaffolding can help.

For rounding a frequently mishandled quantity like 2647 to the nearest hundred, ask, "How many tens for half a hundred? Do we have more or less than five tens? Since we have less than half a hundred, what should we do with the tens and ones? What should take their place?"

A variety of estimation approaches should be encouraged to accompany calculator computations. *Estimation is the calculator check, but do it first.*

How much is half of 10? How much is one more than half of 10? How much is one less than half of 10?

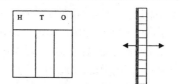

How much is half of 100? How much is one more than half of 100? How much is one less than half of 100?

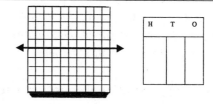

17 The kind of estimations we make depend upon the purpose of the computation or use of the value. Sometimes, just front-ended estimation (using the highest place value) is good enough. If the attendance at a series game is 10,346 on Day 1 and 12,765 on Day 2, it may be good enough to estimate 10,000 and 12,000 for a 2,000-person difference—even though conventional rounding would produce a different figure. If I were estimating the sum of 1,438 and 1,247 to the nearest hundred, I would estimate it as 2,700, quickly noting that the sum of the tens would be close to 100 and adding that to the sum of the hundreds without thinking rounding. If the numbers were rotely rounded to the nearest hundred first, the estimate would have been 2,600.

18
**
23 There are several transitions in the development of the concepts for addition. Some children will quickly move through them or skip them entirely. Others will need more time and manipulative experience or drill and practice. At first, children see addition as an increase in the number line. When confronted with a "How many more?" problem, they will not add on to the last number counted and simply start from one again and count all, including the added value. Once students realize that the last number counted represents a total group or have attained the cardinal principle, they are ready to add on from the last number counted. Teachers can help make this happen by scaffolding sequences such as this:

Count the candies. How many candies did you count? Cover the candies with your paper. How many candies are there? Let's add on three more on top of the paper. How many are under the paper? How many do we have all together?

See Numbers 1-4 for additional counting activities.

Change each value to one half the size.

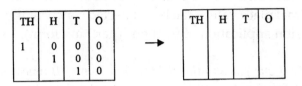

Look at the values in the box below. Put an X over the values in the tens place that are more than half of 100. Circle the values in the hundreds place that are more than half of 1,000. Round the first number to the nearest 1,000. Round the second number to the nearest 100.

TH	H	T	O		TH	H	T	O
8	3	7	8					
2	6	4	2					

Jamie had two computer games, but she got seven more for Christmas. The two-sided chips show them all. How many does she have now?

How did you get your answer? Did anyone count in a different way? What is the easiest way to count them?

2 + 7 = _____   7 + 2 = _____

    Solomon, P. *The Math We Need to "Know" and "Do": Content Standards for Elementary and Middle Grades.* © 2001. Corwin Press, Inc.

23   When solving problems in addition, students will at first follow the sequence of the problem: counting on from the first quantity mentioned (COF) and disregarding the possibilities of an easier approach. For example, they will add 8 to 2 by starting with the 2 instead of adding the 2 to the 8.

Before students can move to the next step of counting on from the largest quantity (COL), they may need to see the quantities as individual wholes or parts that can be combined into a new whole—and recognize that they can be combined in any order (commutative principle of addition).

Problem-solving activities with the bead frame, two-sided chips, and the shoebox roll all work well here. Students can discover as they flip chip sides that, for the same whole, as the number of red sides increases, the yellows decrease and vice versa. Scaffolds include the following:

How big was Jon's part? How big was Mark's part? Put them together. How many do they have all together? Can you put them together in a different way?

Let the students build their own shoebox rolls using a computer-based drawing program. Then, let them invent other graphic ways to show combinations of parts joined to form wholes.

Jane and Lisa each had some baseballs to bring to the game for their team. Jane had six and Lisa had three. Put a circle around Jane's baseballs. Draw Lisa's baseballs in the box. How many did they have together?

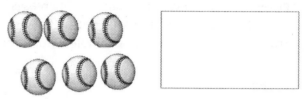

April and Meg are on another team. Meg had four baseballs and April had six. Draw April's baseballs in the box. How many baseballs did Meg and April have together?

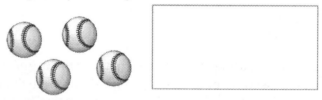

Explain why both teams had the same whole number of baseballs when they got to the game.
Fill in the blanks in the number sentences.
6 + 4 = _____   4 + _____ = 10

Roll the pom-poms for combinations of 10.

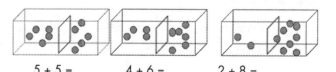

5 + 5 = _____   4 + 6 = _____   2 + 8 = _____

Draw the pom-poms to match the number sentence.

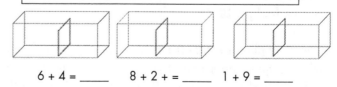

6 + 4 = _____   8 + 2 + = _____   1 + 9 = _____

---

23 The equalities concept—that in order to keep the same size whole, a change in size in one part requires a change in the other—should be clarified before going on to further regrouping concepts. If one part increases in size, then the other decreases, and vice versa. This is also an opportunity to automatize the valuable combinations of 10.

23
**
24 An understanding of part/part whole can then be extended to the possibility of different groupings of more than two parts to form the same whole (associative principle). Color tiles work to show three parts with three different colors. Activities with the balance will reinforce the concept.

How many different ways can we use red, green, and yellow tiles to make a total of 7, 8, 9, and 10? What happens when we trade a yellow for a red?

I have different packages of Popsicle™ sticks. They have 12, 8, 6, 4, or 2 sticks in them. How can I balance one package of 12?

Regrouping an addend into smaller parts to make adding easier is a valuable skill that should follow quickly. Begin with a real problem.

There are four students from one class and eight from another who are going on a trip in two minivans. The minivans hold only six students, because children are not allowed in the front. How can we regroup the students to fit?

John got 10 Pokémon cards, in his new package, that he already had. He traded these doubles one at a time for cards he didn't have. Use your two-sided chips to make a record of his trades from the new package. Turn one chip over for each trade.

John traded for one new card and still had _____ doubles.

John traded for three new cards and still had _____ doubles.

John traded for six new cards and still had _____ doubles.

Explain what happened to the number of new cards and the number of doubles whenever John traded.
Why did they always add up to 1_____0?
Can you think of other parts that would add up to 10?

Cindy loved tee shirts. Her favorite colors were blue, red, and yellow. She had 13 shirts. How many yellow shirts did she have if she had 4 blue ones and six red ones? Use your colored tiles to discover new ideas.

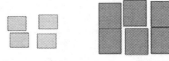 ?

4 blues + 6 reds + _____ yellows = 13 shirts.

Can you think of other combinations of blue, red, and yellow shirts that would add up to 13?
Can you think of combinations of just blue and yellow shirts that would add up to 13?
Why do three parts sometimes add up to same amount as two parts?
Can you make three parts out of these two? (8 + 5)
Can you think of why it may be useful to change two parts into three parts?

25 The ability to regroup addends to form the easily memorized combinations of 10 is a useful number sense skill. Provide practice with the bead frame and use missing addend number sentences. Think about the following:

$8 + 2 + 7 = \square$; $10 + \square = 17$; $8 + 9 = \square$

How is the first problem like the second and the third?

Later, let students discover the value of regrouping for multidigit addition.

$27 + 8 = 27 + 3 + 5$ and
$27 + 38 = 20 + 30 + 7 + 3 + 5$
and then $= 20 + 30 + 7 + 8$
or $= 20 + 30 + 15 = 65$

26 The shift to double-digit addition rarely causes a problem
** if place value understandings are strong (see Numbers
28 12-15). The first critical concepts are that like things must be added to like things, and that numbers in different positions are not like things. Move quickly to three-digit addition without trading.

Some students will not need much time with manipulatives for this transition, but always use the triad of manipulative, words, and written symbols when solving the initial problems. Use packages of Popsicle™ sticks or base 10 blocks. Place these on back sheets of tens and ones columns. Later, it may be useful to let students prove their answers to others by demonstrating with manipulatives.

Front-end estimation should precede exact calculations. Students can discover that the sum of two two-digit numbers will have to be the same or larger than the sum of the tens-place digits.

Stacey had eight playstation games and Anna had five. How many did they have together? Try making tens. $8 + 5 = 8 + 2 + 3 = ?$

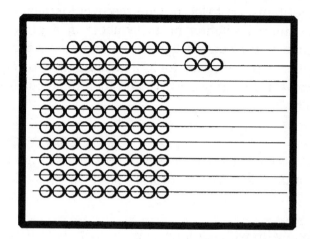

Sour balls came in packages of 10. Jane had 2 packages of grape balls and 3 loose grape balls. How many grape balls did she have? She also had 3 packages of lemon balls and six loose lemon balls. How many lemon balls did she have? How many sour balls did she have altogether? How did you find your answer? Did you add the packages or the loose ones first? Does it make a difference? Evan had 43 lemon sour balls and 35 strawberry balls. About how many sour balls did he have? Would a good estimate be more than 70? Why? Use your Popsicle™ sticks to show us how you got your answer.

29 The concept of *trading* (sometimes called regrouping) replaces (and makes more sense than) *borrowing*. Trading is critical to an understanding of all common operation algorithms. Try to let students discover for themselves the structural limitation of 10 symbols in a place in our number system. And then let them discover the trading option. Use the calculator as a manipulative to help them discover this, or use a two- and then three-part shoebox roll.

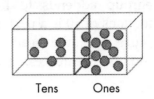

Tens Ones

How many pom-poms are there in each side of our shoebox? Can you write this total in our number system symbol form? What would we have to do with the pom-poms in our shoebox to make it like our number system?

How can we make our shoebox like our number system? What should we do if there are 10 pom-poms in the ones place?

Kelly had 17 hits before this game, and she got 6 more. How many does she have altogether? Show how you got your answer with your powers-of-10 blocks and complete the number sentence.

Follow up with addition activities with base 10 blocks or packages of Popsicle™ sticks. Use a back sheet that indicates tens and ones or hundreds, tens, and ones. Always accompany the manipulative operation with the symbolic form. You may even try trading in systems that are other than base 10 to reinforce the multiple representation idea. Baseball cards and other popular trading cards are possible connections. Once students have constructed the trading concept as a practical way to handle numbers, move quickly to the hundreds place.

Once the concept is clearly developed, children may not wish to bother with the manipulatives, and they become cumbersome with large numbers—even distracting from the concept. Let them use the symbolic form, but from time to time ask them to prove their answers with the manipulatives. Use manipulatives again at the beginning of transitions to the next larger place value.

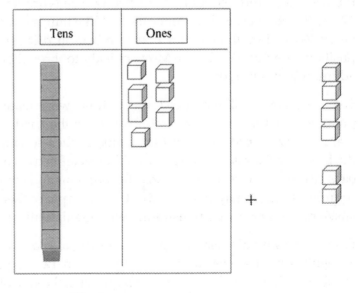

Tens	Ones

$17 + 6 =$ _____

30 Identification of the patterns created when the same number is added repeatedly (addition series) can be useful in developing number sense. Try building geometric forms to match the series to see the pattern connections.

Build three triangles with your blocks. Make the bottom row one block larger each time. What happens to the total number of blocks each time?

31
**
33 Subtraction presents the first great challenge for some students. The first subtraction concept, counting backward on the number line, is easily followed by a transition to subtraction as "take away." The difficulty arises because problems that require the subtraction operation do not all involve take away. Students who understand traditional or canonical take-away problems find it more difficult to solve noncanonical problems that involve comparison and problems where the result is given but the change or start is not known. It may be wise to move more quickly beyond take away and think of subtraction as *finding the difference.*

The concept of *inequalities* may be a good way to introduce the finding-the-difference concept. Children are always comparing things, and it may be a natural approach. The balance beam is excellent for inequalities, and it allows a focus on subtraction as finding the difference.

Eight is greater than five, 8 > 5. How are eight chips and five chips different? What do you have to do to make them balance? The difference between 8 and 5 is 3, but can you make the values equal in more than one way (either by adding three to the smaller or taking away three from the larger)?

When subtraction is a comparison between two wholes, the concept is clearly to find the difference, but it can be used for other problems as well.

Find the difference.
Balance the scale.

$8 - 3 =$ _____

$3 +$ _____ $= 8$

31 At the upper grades, inequality problems that involve a
** known sum and difference, but unknown parts or addends,
33 can then be solved as an extended variation of the above.

31 Relating the subtraction operation to the part/part whole relationship, *subtraction is when you know the whole and one part but not the other part. The unknown part is the difference between the whole and the part you know.* Even take-away problems can be described with this concept.

Sally had eight computer games. She gave three to her friend Jane. What is the whole that Sally had before she gave any away? What is the part she gave to Jane? What is the part she has left? What is the difference between what she had before and now?

The finding-the-difference concept also works for the noncanonical start unknown problem. For example:

John has 11 action figures. He got four for Christmas. How many did he have before Christmas? What is John's whole number of action figures? What is the part he got for Christmas? How can we find the other part, the part he had before Christmas? What is the difference between the number he had before and after Christmas?

It also works for the change unknown problem.

Judy has 27 action figures. She had 19 before Christmas. How many did she get for Christmas? What is Judy's whole number of action figures? What is the part she had before Christmas? How can we find the other part, the part she got for Christmas? What is the difference between the number she had before and after Christmas?

The sum of two numbers is 27, and the difference between them is three. If you take off the difference and put an equal amount of what is left on each side of the balance, how many will be on each side? How can you then make only one side larger by the difference? What are the two values?

James used 20 tracks for his train setup. Sixteen of them were straight tracks. How many were curved?
THINK: How many tracks in the whole setup? How many in the straight part? What is the difference between the number of tracks in the whole setup, and the number of straight tracks?

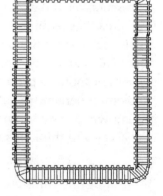

Complete the number sentence:

20 – 16 = _____

Evan collected rock specimens and kept them in a special box that he bought with 22 specimens already inside. He now has 34 specimens in his box. How many specimens has he collected since he bought his box?
THINK: What is the difference between what he had at first and what he has now?

Complete the number sentences:

22 + _____ = 34

34 – 22 = _____

Rocks

31   Students will need to discover that unlike addition, the subtraction operation is not commutative, and it is common practice to subtract the smaller value from the larger value. However, they should discover that sometimes, it is easier to count up in a subtraction problem than it is to count down. The take-away concept makes this transition of making the easier choice difficult, but subtraction as "finding the difference" helps.

Sandy had eight fish in her tank and she gave Fran six. How many did she have left? How did you find your answer? Can you think of an easier way? What she had left was the difference between what she had at the beginning and what she had after she gave the fish away. Suppose she had 18 fish and gave away 16. What would be the easiest way to find the difference?

35   Related subtraction and addition facts through 20 should
**   be automatized before moving to multidigit subtraction
37   with trading. If place value concepts and trading ideas are well developed for addition, the transition to subtraction with trading should not present a problem. Like things have to be subtracted from like things, and if we do not have the like things, we can trade. Base 10 blocks and Popsicle™ sticks are excellent for concept development. *The transition from using concrete materials* to using just the symbolic form of the subtraction algorithm, however, is sometimes difficult because there is a tendency, with the concrete materials in front of them, for students to take away the units one by one and count the remainder instead of relying on mentally automatized combinations. This is not possible in the algorithm. In preparation for transition to the algorithm, have the students hide their manipulatives and predict remainders before they count, and then let them check their predictions.

What is the easiest way to find the difference between 8 and 11? Can you think of a problem that makes you find the difference between 8 and 11? Write a number sentence for finding the difference between 8 and 11.

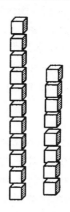

How would you find the difference between 28 and 31?

Write a number sentence for this.

The baseball cards Roger bought came in packages of 10. He bought three packages of cards to add to the three single ones that he already had. Then gave 16 of his 33 cards to his friend Sam for his birthday. How many cards did Roger have left? Write a vertical number sentence for this problem and use your base 10 blocks to help solve it. You will need to trade for more ones. Before you take any of Sam's cards away, predict how many single ones will be left for Roger.

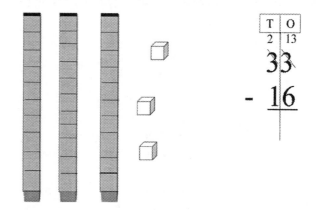

37 One of the most challenging hurdles in learning the subtraction operation using only the rote algorithm is subtracting across zeros. Using base 10 blocks or the shoebox roll, students can see more easily that, as in the problem illustrated, the 100 is a source for needed ones, but it is more practical to trade first for the tens and then for the ones. Careful connections between the manipulative and the symbolic form will help.

Use a triad of connecting the concrete manipulative or real object to the words, and then to the symbols, and then back again. The take-away concept works best in the transition to trading in the common algorithm.

We don't have enough ones. Where can we get them? We don't have tens, but we do have hundreds. Can we trade hundreds for ones? How many ones can we get for 100? It is too much trouble to count out 100 ones, so can you think of an easier way to trade? If we trade 100 for 10 tens, how many hundreds do we have left? How many tens will we have? Where can we get the ones we need? How many tens will be left? How many ones?

Let's write everything we just did in symbol form. Explain what each symbol means.

Jamal had 103 pages to read in his book. He finished seven pages in his silent reading time. How many more pages does he have to go? Use your blocks to solve the problem and then describe what happens in the symbol form.

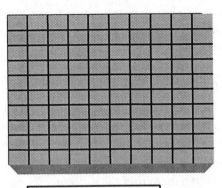

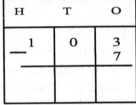

How many ones did you have to take away to find the difference?
How many did you have? How could you get more?
Why couldn't you get them from the tens? Where did you get them from? What did you do first?
How many hundreds did you have left? Then what did you do?
How many tens did you have left? Then what did you do?
Explain all your steps. Show them in symbol form.

Now subtract 7 from 1,003.

38
**
39

There are a number of transitions in the development of multiplication concepts that will occur over time as related concepts. Skip counting (see #9) has to progress from the rote repetition of sequence number names through the idea of skipping numbers as we count, and then to the idea that each time we skip count, we are adding another unit or group of two, three, or four—or the repeated addition of the same value. The mathematical language of "times" needs connections to "the number of times a unit value is repeated."

What is another way to say three repeated four times? Three, three, three, and three is four times three and shown by the symbols 4 X (3). How can we describe the symbols 6 X (2) in words? How can we show this on our bead frame?

It may also be useful to introduce the place value concepts for multiples of 10 that are described in #14 at the same time that beginning ideas in multiplication are approached. Connect also to repeated units of measures of area.

Doubling of the units can follow quickly and may reinforce the conceptual ideas. Start with doubling the number of times a group or unit is repeated: Two fives are 10, so how much would four fives be?

$2 \times (5) = 10$
$4 \times (5) = ?$

Then, move to doubling the size of the group: If four threes are twelve, then how much are four sixes?

$4 \times (3) = 12$
$4 \times (6) = $ question

Bead frames are very helpful here, but also use arrays of chips and colored tiles.

Mike mowed his neighbor's lawn for a month. He got four dollars each time he mowed the lawn, and he mowed three times. How many dollars did he earn? Show how many *times* the four dollars are repeated on the bead frame. Tell your partner about how you got your answer. Write a number sentence for this problem.

This number sentence describes how much Mike earned for the whole summer: $6 \times (4) = $ _____

Tell your partner how many times Mike mowed the lawn that summer. Show this on your bead frame. Tell your partner how to get to the answer. Compare how much Mike earned for one month with how much he earned for the summer.

Jill scored six points for each challenge the first time she played her video game. How many points did she score for four challenges? With practice she got even better, and scored twice as much the next time she played. Show the first game score on your bead frame, then the second game score. Write a number sentence for each. What is the easiest way to get your answer for the second game?

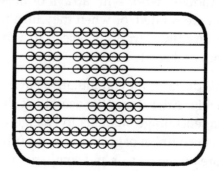

39
**
40

The *number of times* a value is repeatedly added is an abstract operand on the value. In the addition operation, you are combining concrete parts to form the whole, and each value is represented concretely. In multiplication, a single concrete value is repeated a certain number of times. Consider three fours. The four is represented concretely, but there is no array of size three. Thus, when using symbolic number sentences for multiplication, some teachers find it helpful to unitize the repeated unit by placing it in parentheses. Three fours are symbolized as 3 × (4), and four threes are 4 × (3). Although commutatively, the totals are equal, the concept connection to what is described by these symbolic forms is different—and it will be describing a different problem. The commutative principle of multiplication is very helpful in automatization of facts but may be a deterrent to early meaning making of the multiplication concept.

Organizing the repetitions into tables and geometric representations with colored tiles can help with the recognition of patterns and automatization. Begin using the tables for pattern discoveries other than commutation, and then shift to commutation.

41

The commutative principle of multiplication is best discovered as students work with arrays of objects like colored tiles that are rotated, or when they turn the bead frame. They can also draw arrays of objects in a computer drawing program and rotate them.

Then, let students discover the commutative pattern on the multiplication table. After doing the activity at the top of the next column, encourage students to change the table notations so that the number of groups is on the (y) axis and the repetitions are on the (x) axis and compare the tables.

SIZE OF GROUP		(0)	(1)	(2)	(3)	(4)	(5)	(6)	(7)	(8)	(9)	(10)
	0x	0	0	0	0	0	0	0	0	0	0	0
	1x	0	1	2	3	4	5	6	7	8	9	10
	2x	0	2	4	6	8	10	12	14	16	18	20
NUMBER	3x	0	3	6	9	12	15	18	21	24	27	30
OF TIMES A GROUP	4x	0	4	8	12	16	20	24	28	32	36	40
IS	5x	0	5	10	15	20	25	30	35	40	45	50
REPEATED	6x	0	6	12	18	24	30	36	42	48	54	60
	7x	0	7	14	21	28	35	42	49	56	63	70
	8x	0	8	16	24	32	40	48	56	64	72	80
	9x	0	⁵	18	27	36	45	54	63	72	81	90
	10x	0	10	20	30	40	50	60	70	80	90	100

Compare 2 × (4) and 4 × (4).
Compare 3 × (3) and 6 × (3).
Compare 2 × (3) and 2 × (6).
How many other doubles can you find?
Why are there two rows of zeros?

Jerry and Adam brought some marshmallows for the party. One of them put two marshmallows in each of six baskets, and the other put six marshmallows in each of two baskets. How many marshmallows did each friend bring? Who put the marshmallows in six baskets?
Finish the number sentence for this problem.
What is the same about what Jerry and Adam did? What is different?

$$2 \times 6 = \underline{\hspace{1cm}}$$

$$6 \times \underline{\hspace{1cm}} = 12$$

42
**
43

Multiplication can also be conceptualized as enlargement. See #14 and #15, as well as their corresponding activities, for an explanation of this.

The pattern of a left shift of place value for multiplication in our number system is also described in the sections listed above. It should precede the following.

The generalizations that 20 X 40 is twice as much as 10 times 40 and that two tens times four tens is eight hundreds are important pattern recognitions to accompany multidigit multiplication. They can be used to estimate problems and build number sense. Tables can help students see this pattern. Manipulatives, however, should be used to introduce the tables. Base 10 blocks are helpful with smaller values, but then grid sheets of tens or play money may be more practical.

Gina has 20 dollars. She needs 10 times as much for her computer game. How much is 10 twenties? She needs 20 times as much for a new printer. How much is 20 times 20? She needs 50 times as much for a new computer. How much is that? Count all of these with your play money and then find the operation on the table. What is another way to think of 50 times 20?

Number of times a group is repeated	0x	1x	2x	3x	4x	5x	6x	7x	8x	9x	10x
0	0	0	0	0	0	0	0	0	0	0	0
1	0	1	2	3	4	5	6	7	8	9	10
2	0	2	4	6	8	10	12	14	16	18	20
3	0	3	6	9	12	15	18	21	24	27	30
4	0	4	8	12	16	20	24	28	32	36	40
5	0	5	10	15	20	25	30	35	40	45	50
6	0	6	12	18	24	30	36	42	48	54	60
7	0	7	14	21	28	35	42	49	56	63	70
8	0	8	16	24	32	40	48	56	64	72	80
9	0	9	18	27	36	45	54	63	72	81	90
10	0	10	20	30	40	50	60	70	80	90	100

(Row labels on left: "Size of the group (unit)")

Compare this table with the one you used before. How are they the same? How are they different?

Put a circle around the number 27. What did it mean on the first table? What does it mean on this table?

How can the tables help you remember the multiplication combinations?

Why can we say "If you know 20, then you know plenty?"

Number of times a group is repeated	0x	10x	20x	30x	40x	50x
0	0	0	0	0	0	0
10	0	100	200	300	400	500
20	0	200	400	600	800	1000
30	0	300	600	900	1200	1500
40	0	400	800	1200	1600	2000
50	0	500	1000	1500	2000	2500
60	0	600	1200	1800	2400	3000
70	0	700	1400	2100	2800	3500
80	0	800	1600	2400	3200	4000
90	0	900	1800	2700	3600	4500
100	0	1000	2000	3000	4000	5000
1000						

(Row labels on left: "Size of the group (unit)")

Compare this table with the one you used before.

How much is 3 tens times 6 tens? How much is 4 tens times 5 tens?

Do you see a pattern? Think about larger numbers that are not on this table. How much would 4 tens times 5 hundreds be?

$60 \times 300 =$ _____ $400 \times 30 =$ _____

Finish the last row of this table. Add a 200x column.

44
**
46

Multidigit multiplication requires several conceptual tranitions.

1. The critical concept is that if each digit is repeatedly added separately and then the products are combined, the total is equivalent to repeated addition of both digits. Essentially, adding (23) four times to get 92 is the same as adding (20) four times to get 80 and (3) four times to get 12 and then combining the partial products to get 92. This is the distributive principle of multiplication.

2. A good way to begin is by just asking for front-end estimation and then asking for the exact amount. 23 x 41 is about two tens times four tens or 800. This will push students toward the estimation habit and better number sense. Starting with the tens is different from the common algorithm where we begin with the ones, but students can discover that either sequence works.

3. Start with single-digit multipliers and double-digit multiplicands.

4. Trading should not be a problem if the concept has been developed with addition. Use base 10 blocks at the start of concept development or grid sheets and money. Make the triad connections of manipulatives, words, and symbols.

5. Gradually get students to combine the separate calculations into one vertical form. A shift in thinking may be necessary for translation to the vertical form. First of all, the convention in horizontal form is to state the operand (the number of times) first. In the vertical form, the repeated unit comes first.

Shanequa had a collection of CDs. She kept them on racks. Each rack held 24 CDs. How many CDs could she stack on four racks? About how many did each rack hold? About how much would four racks hold? Let's write that as a number sentence. 4 X 20 = 80. How many more could each rack actually hold? How many can four racks hold? How many is that? Let's write a number sentence for that: 4 X 4 = 16. How many CDs can the four racks hold altogether? Explain how we got the answer.

Marla earned 45 dollars for babysitting in one week. She babysat for the same time for each of three weeks. How much did she earn in all three weeks?
Estimate your answer first, then do this problem with your group.

What does the picture show? How many tens did she earn for three weeks? How much money is that? How did you get that answer? How many ones did she earn in three weeks? Complete the number sentences that describe parts of problem. What is inside the parentheses?

_____ × (4 × 10) = _____   or   _____ × 40 = _____

_____ × (5 × 1) = _____   or   _____ × 5 = _____

What do you have to do to show the whole amount she earned? Could you count the ones first? Complete the number sentence for the whole problem:

(3 × 40) + (3 × 5) = 3 × 45 = _____

47
**
48
Before introducing double-digit multipliers, it may be helpful for students to review the concept (see #43) that 20 times a quantity is twice as much as 10 times that quantity, and then discover that we can either make the quantity 10 times larger and then make it twice as large or make it twice as large and then 10 times larger (the associative principle: $3 \times 10 \times 2$ is equal to $3 \times 2 \times 10$).

At first, use grid sheets or base 10 blocks to develop this concept, or graphics computer programs. Balloons can work as well! Then, shift to symbols and use the left shift with either sequence. How can we make (37) 20 times larger? Can we make it 10 times larger? Now, how can we make it 20 times larger? Can we make it two times larger first?

Allow students to discover how to combine the partial products of the two steps in the algorithm, multiplying by the digit value and shifting one place to the left for 10 times—or more for larger multiples of 10.

Opposite is a step-by-step scaffolding that may help introduce the standard algorithm. Students should work in groups to solve the problem and analyze the algorithm. Let them suggest ways to improve it or alternates.

For larger multipliers (operands) and multiplicands (unit or group), the final generalizations that tens times tens are equal to hundreds and tens times hundreds are equal to thousands should be encouraged. They are efficient and will be important for estimations of multiplication problems and as an inverse for estimation of division problems.

Sean had a regular job cutting lawns. He made $35 a week. How much did he make in the 23-week season? Show this problem in horizontal and in vertical form Estimate your answer, then use your play money to get the exact answer.

$23 \times$ _____ = _____

$$\begin{array}{r} 35 \\ \times\ 23 \\ \hline \end{array}$$

Use your play money to get the exact answer.
A. How many of these for each week?
B. How many for 3 weeks?
C. How many for 20 weeks?
D. How many for 23 weeks?
E. How much money is that?
F. How many of these for each week?
G. How many for 3 weeks?
H. How many for 10 weeks?
I. How many for 23 weeks?
J. How how much money is that?

$23 \times 5 =$ _____ $23 \times 30 =$ _____

How much did Sean earn in 23 weeks?

Here is one kind of algorithm that is use for multiplication problems like Sean's. Explain it to your group. Do you know another algorithm you can use? Can you make this one better?

	3	⑤
x	△2	⟨3⟩

1	5	Write the letter of the question that this line answers.❏
9	0	Write the letter of the question that this line answers.❏
1 0	0	Write the letter of the question that this line answers.❏
6 0	0	Write the letter of the question that this line answers.❏

Write the letter of the question that this line answers
AND ANSWER IT.❏

Now try this.
Write a number sentence for the product of the values in the hexagon and the circle.
Write a number sentence for the product of the values in the square and the hexagon.
Write a number sentence for the product of the values in the triangle and the circle.
Write a number sentence for the product of the values in the triangle and the square.

49 Cartesian multiplication requires the computation of the product of factors but is conceptually different from repeated addition or enlargement. The possible number of combinations of two skirts and three blouses can be shown visually with tree diagrams and is the product of the number of skirts and blouses or $2 \times 3 = 6$ (see Numbers 195 and 196 for other combination problems).

Randy had two backpacks and four caps that he wore to school. He changed the combinations often, using a different cap and different pack, but always wore a cap and carried a pack. How many different combinations of packs and caps could he get? Make a tree diagram to help you find out.

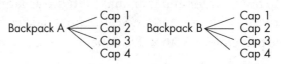

50 Multiplication tables can be an introduction to multiplication series and functions. Try the symbolic notation for the four table. $N = n \times (4)$, where N = each value and n is the ordinal number in a series. The value of the fifth number in the four table is 5×4 or 20. The patterns of multiplication can be observed in many ways. Make connections to the area of rectangles. Use color tiles to allow students to discover what happens when one side is increased a unit, when both sides are increased, and when the sides are doubled. Examine squares and introduce the square notation.

4×4 4×5 5×5 4×8

51
**
53
Just as subtraction presents the first great hurdle for students in the early elementary grades, division presents a challenge for the upper grades. Part of the difficulty lies in the variations of the division concepts and the tendency for teachers to overlook these concepts and move too quickly to a difficult algorithm. To begin with, children have a naturally developed understanding of the sharing process or *partition* division. Given real problems and manipulatives, they solve partition problems readily.

We had 12 candy bars after Halloween and wanted to share them among three friends. How many will each friend get?

Children will place the individual bars one by one in each of three piles or may immediately just try to equalize the piles. In a partition problem, we know the whole value and we know the number of parts. What we do not know is the size of each part.

In *quotition** division, we know the size of the group but not the number of groups. Quotition is the inverse of repeated addition and can be explained on a number line as repeated subtraction. Quotition problems are a good way to relate division to multiplication. Use a variety of manipulatives and the calculator to develop these concepts.

We had 12 candy bars and gave four bars to each of our friends. How many friends got four candy bars?
    Enter the whole number of candy bars into your calculator. Subtract four at a time. How many times did you subtract four before you got to zero? How many fours are there in twelve? How many friends got candy bars?

Difficulties with the operation arise when we try to move students from the partition meaning of division to the quotition meaning without careful transitions.

Kim and her friends collected Pokemon cards. They decided to pool their cards and make an album. They counted 115 cards. Each page of the album held 5 cards. How many pages did they fill? Use your base 10 blocks to help you solve this problem. What kind of problem is this? Write a number sentence for this problem.

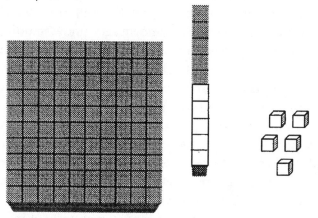

Think about this. How many groups of 5 were there in 10? How many in 100? How many would there be in 1,000? How many fours are there in 12? How many in 120?

*In some texts, quotition is called "measurement" division.

51
**
55

Students should be encouraged to identify the differences in division problems in terms of what is given and what is sought. Although quotition problems are less common to the child's experience, the standard division algorithm has been traditionally taught in the frame of reference of a quotition problem. To encourage understanding, the standard algorithm and inventive procedures should be explored within a triad of problem words, manipulatives, and symbols in the context of both partition and quotition problems. Teachers will find some of the triad connections different and perhaps more difficult with quotition (even though we traditionally use its terms in teaching the algorithm). For example, trading makes better sense in partition problems than in quotition problems. For example, in the division of 201 by 3 ($201 \div 3$) we cannot divide two hundreds into three equal parts of hundreds, and so we trade for tens. Thinking quotition, on the other hand, we know that there are at least 60 groups of 3 in 200, but not 70. The estimation approach and recognition of patterns such as those in the figure on the previous page will help.

Angelo had 62 pieces of gum for his party. The gum came in packages of five. How many whole packages did he have? Did he have any loose ones? What was the whole amount of gum?

What does the problem tell us? Are we trying to find out the number of parts (packages of gum) or the size of each group? Will there be more or less than 10 packages? How do you know? How many pieces in 10 packages? How many more pieces do we have over the 10 packages? How many fives in 12? How many whole packages do we have altogether? How many loose pieces?

We wanted to share 85 chuckles equally among six children. The chuckles came in packages of 10. How many whole packages of 10 (tens) would each one get? How many extra, undivided packages of 10 would there be? What will we have to do with the extra packages? How many single chuckles (ones) would we have now? If we divide the rest of the single chuckles among the six children, how many will each one get? How many chuckles would they have in all?

Keshawn and his three friends teamed up to earn money by making deliveries for the store. They earned $96.00 one day and divided it equally amongst themselves. How much did each friend earn? Show this problem as a number sentence and as an algorithm.

$96 \div \underline{\quad} = ?$ $\underline{\quad} \overline{| 96}$ Estimate your answer, then use your play money to get the exact answer.

A. How many of these can be evenly divided among the four friends?
B. How much will each friend get?
C. How much of the whole amount of money does that use up?
D. How can the remaining money be divided amongst the friends?

E. What has to be added to these?
F. How many of these will there be after the traded 10 ones are added?
G. How many of these can you give to each friend?
H. How much money does this use up?

$90 \div 4 = \underline{\quad} + ?$ $(6 + 10) \div 4 = \underline{\quad}$

Here is one kind of algorithm that is used for division problems like Keshawn's. Explain it to your group. Do you know another algorithm you can use? Can you make this one better?

 Write the letter of the question in the box that the value in the circle answers. ☐
Write the letter of the question in the box that the value in the triangle answers. ☐

4 | 9 6
  8 0   Write the letter of the question in the box that this line answers. ☐
  1 6   Write the letter of the question in the box that this line answers. ☐
  1 6   Write the letter of the question in the box that this line answers. ☐
  0 0   Explain what this means.

56   Partition division is related to fractions and the connection should be made immediately. If you divide one whole into three parts, each part is one third of the whole. Translate one form into another and finally reach the generalization that the fraction form can represent the division process. One third represents one whole divided into three parts, and two thirds is two wholes divided into three parts (see #69).

57   Automatization of division facts is a critical precursor to
**   the mastery of a division algorithm. Manipulatives and
61   tables will help students recognize the patterns. Use both the partition and quotition concepts for these.

If there are four sixes in 24, how many threes will there be? If we divide 32 into four parts, and each part is size eight, how big will each part be if we divide the 32 into 8 parts?

Once the facts are automatized, estimation of quotients for multidigit divisor problems is both possible and useful. Allow students to use a variety of approaches to the estimation process, but the inverse generalization to the one for multidigit multiplication is very useful. If tens times hundreds are thousands (e.g., 2 tens times 3 hundreds are 6 thousands), then thousands divided by tens are hundreds, and thousands divided by hundreds are tens ($21{,}000 \div 70 = 300$ and $21{,}000 \div 700 = 30$). Twenty-one thousands divided by 7 tens = 3 hundreds, and 21 thousands divided by 7 hundreds = 3 tens.

Ten pencils were shared among five students. How many pencils did each student get? What fractional part of the whole number of pencils did each student get? How many pencils is that equal to?

$10 \div 5 =$ ____   ____ of 10 = 2

Size of part or number of parts	10	20	30	40	50
Size of part or number of parts 100	1000	2000	3000	4000	5000
200	2000	4000	6000	8000	10000
300	3000	6000	9000	12000	15000
400	4000	8000	12000	16000	2000
500	5000	10000	15000	20000	25000
600	6000	12000	18000	24000	30000
700	7000	14000	21000	28000	35000
800	8000	16000	24000	32000	40000
900	9000	18000	27000	36000	45000
1000	10000	20000	30000	40000	50000
2000	20000	40000	60000	80000	100000

Use this table to help estimate the following division problems:

5,976 books were placed on 30 library shelves. How many books were placed on each shelf?

59,045 books were stacked in the library with 2,000 books in each section. How many sections were filled?

For each problem, describe what information you were given and what you had to find out.

Compare the two problems. How are they different? How are they the same?

Do you see any patterns?

Think about larger numbers that are not on the table. Add another row.

60 It is easy for students to understand that zero divided into any number of parts is still going to be zero, or that there are no other quantities in zero.

However, dividing a number value by zero is more of an abstraction and difficult to understand. When any number is divided by zero, the quotient is undefined. The problem may lie in the way we describe the division problem. From the quotitive perspective, when we ask, "How many twos are there in six?" we infer *the most* number of twos. For example, there could be (1) two and (1) four, or (2) twos and (2) ones in six, but the most number of twos in six is three. There is really no limit to the number of zeros in a sum value of six, and so we say that six divided by zero is undefined. Real data such as that in the figure opposite is useful.

The following table shows the number of runs (RBIs) for each baseball team that was the total for several games. For each team, decide what is the greatest number of innings where there could have been two RBIs, the greatest number of innings where there could have been three runs, and the greatest number of innings where there could have been zero runs.

Team	Total RBIs	Most possible innings with two runs	Most possible innings with three runs	Most possible innings with zero runs
Team A	24			
Team B	36			

How did you get your answers for the greatest number of innings with two runs and the greatest number with three runs?

Why was it impossible to get an answer for the greatest number of innings with zero runs? Give some possibilities for how different numbers of zero RBI innings could be scored in one game with a score of 12 runs.

Why is any number divided by zero undefined?

61 Once students can use and explain the standard algorithm and estimate answers with ease, it may be unnecessary to spend a great deal of time practicing multidigit, long division algorithms.

My suggestion for algorithm practice is a set of 10 problems—all estimated first. The first three should then be completed without a calculator. If the answers are all correct, then the rest should be done with the calculator. If there is a mistake on the first three, then the student should correct it and do three more without the calculator. Any additional mistakes should be followed by three problems without the calculator until three problems are done correctly.

For the division problem of 24,345 ÷ 81, will the answer be closer to 3000, 300, or 30? Explain your estimate. Suppose the divisor was 89, would the answer be more or less than 300? More or less than 200? Why?

62
**
66

Children develop beginning concepts of fractions at a relatively early age. They understand "half of it" as something less than a whole, but they may not understand one half as the name of one part of something that has been divided into two equal parts. The next cloudy concept is the recognition that the name "one half," or any fraction name, describes only the quantity in relation to the whole rather than a definitive quantity. In other words, the amount of something that can be described as "half" depends on the size of the whole.

The next important concept is that the relative quantity of one part of the same whole decreases with the number of parts. A hurdle to overcome is that an increasing denominator represents smaller relative amounts, but experiences that emphasize the concept that a greater number of parts results in smaller pieces of the same whole are useful. As this concept is constructed, review the idea that for unit fractions to be compared easily, they must be parts of the same whole. One half of a large pie is not the same as ½ of a small pie. One third of a large pie is smaller than one half of a large pie, but it may not be smaller than ½ of a small pie.

It may be a good idea to move quickly from the concept of unit fractional parts of whole things to the partition division relationship of parts of groups of things. The potato chip bag problem opposite allows students to make the connections between the related concepts (also see the pencils problem on page 91).

Eventually, students should reach the generalization that in order to find a unit fractional part of a number, you divide by the denominator.

At the movies, Jane and Alice decided to buy and share one candy bar. What part of the candy bar would each girl get? Which would you prefer, one half of the candy bar in the circle, or one half of the candy bar outside of the circle? Why?

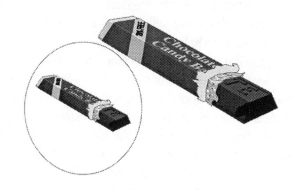

Matt and his friends shared a small bag of potato chips. (Altogether there were four people sharing.) What is the fraction name for the part of the bag that each friend received?

The next time the four friends were together they bought a large size bag. What is the fraction name for the part of the bag each friend received? Did they get the same amount each time? Explain your answer.
What would the friends have to do to know exactly how many chips were in one fourth of the small and large size bags?

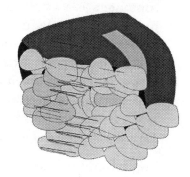

64
**
68   The transition to more-than-unit fractions for single wholes does not usually present a problem—except perhaps in the verbalization of what the numerator and denominator represent. Identification of the denominator as the number of parts into which the whole has been divided should be established clearly in experiences with unit fractions. The most common way to describe the numerator is that it represents the number of parts of the whole we are thinking about or have. A good beginning for more-than-unit fractions of wholes may be to strengthen the concepts developed with unit fractions by scaffolding the alternate fraction names for wholes and comparing them. For example, $7/7 = 6/6 = 5/5 = 4/4 = 3/3 = 2/2 = 1$ of the same whole. Connections to real problems are best for this concept.

Then, move to unit fractions of sets. *How did we find out what one third of 12 is? If one third of 12 is 4, then how can we find out how much two thirds of 12 are?* Follow this with an introduction to fractions that are more than one whole (improper).

Sometimes, there may be fuzziness about the class inclusion definitions of the total set. It is easy to visualize 10 computers as a whole set or group, but there is a conceptual leap to considering an aquarium with different fish as a whole group of fish and the individual kinds of fish as parts of that whole. After all, the fish are different! Examples of both kinds of wholes or sets are needed. This may also serve as an introduction to set theory. The different kinds of fish are subsets of the whole set but also can be described as fractional parts of the whole.

This introduces, and can be followed quickly by, addition and subtraction operations with like fractions. We can add and subtract like parts. The denominators of like parts are the same relative size of single whole objects or groups.

There were 10 computers in the classroom. What fraction of the whole is each computer? Two of the computers had CD-ROM drives. What fraction of the whole had CD-ROM drives? What fraction did not? How many did not have a CD-ROM drive?

8/10 of 10 = _____

We also had an aquarium in the classroom. What part of our fish were guppies? What part were angel fish?

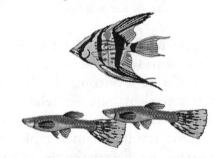

Four friends went for pizza. The pizza pie came sliced into eight pieces. How much pizza could each one get?

8 pieces ÷ 4 parts = _____ pieces

1/4 of 8 pieces = _____ pieces

8/4 of one piece = _____ pieces

BUT

each piece = 1/8 of the whole pie

Each friend will get _____ of the whole pie

68   Relating to the somewhat different concept of division as shrinkage, students should have experiences that help them develop the idea that fractions can be used to describe the relative size of single objects or groups. My favorite example is a reference to the popular movies in which the children are shrunk or enlarged. There is no difference in the number of children, and no one is cut in half. Each child is eight times larger or eight times smaller. A small bag of chips is half the size of a larger bag and may have half the number of chips, but conceptually, there are not two parts—just one that is half the size. The other half is an abstraction.

70   The transition to an understanding of fractions as a representation of parts of a group or set where the number of parts into which the set is to be divided is more than the number of wholes is often overlooked. The first step in this transition is an understanding that even though there is more than one whole, each part is going to be less than one whole.

We have three small pizzas to divide among the four of us. Will we each get more or less than a whole pizza? Explain your answer.

The next step should be the concept that each whole will have to be divided and then the parts combined.

We can't divide the three whole pizzas evenly, so what will we have to do with them? If we divide the three pizzas into the four parts we need, how big a part of each pizza will each of us get? But we have three pizzas, so how much pizza will each of us get in all?

Eventually, this should lead to the generalization that any fraction can represent the operation of numerator divided by the denominator. An extension of this is that a whole number can be expressed as a fraction with a denominator of 1.

Rhonda wanted to study a bug under her microscope. She measured it first with her centimeter ruler. It measured 2 centimeters. Her microscope had a lens that made everything four times larger than it really was. How big would the bug appear to be under the microscope? Then she put another insect on a slide and looked at it. The new bug appeared to be about 4 centimeters. How large was it really?

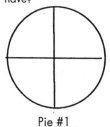

In real life, every thing Rhonda saw through her microscope was _____ (what fraction) of what it appeared to be?

Four friends went for pizza. They bought three large, unsliced pizza pies. Could each friend have one whole pizza? What part of a whole pizza could each have?

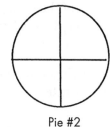 Pie #1   Pie #2   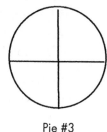 Pie #3

Each friend got _____ of each pie. Altogether it was the same as _____ of a single pie.

Three wholes divided into four parts = _____.

How much would they each receive if there were five friends?

Three wholes divided into five parts = _____.

A group of friends went for pizza. They bought three pies and each had 3/8 of a pie. How many friends were there?

A group of six friends went for pizza. They each had 5/6 of a pie. How many pies did they buy?

70 The concept of simple equivalents can be constructed easily by using real materials. Fraction bars and circles are useful manipulatives to develop these concepts. I prefer the bars for equivalents because the pieces are ordered so that the equivalents are all clearly recognizable as equal parts of the same size whole that can be seen as a referent. Paper folding is also helpful. Students can actually produce equivalents as they fold equal-sized paper sheets into smaller and smaller parts.

One easily overcome limitation of manipulatives is that students see the whole only as a single unit. The whole can also represent a set of individual units. Empty egg cartons filled with cubes, pom-poms, or color tiles with colored threads or pipe cleaners to mark the divisions are effective. Students can see the whole as a unit—the whole dozen carton, and, at the same time, the set of individual units that comprises it. One half of the whole carton is also six eggs. Six twelfths of the whole carton is the same number of eggs as ½ of the carton or ²⁄₄ of the carton. A combination of the bars and the cartons may be the best. You can also try sets of fraction bars and papers.

Some important generalizations should come from experiences with equivalent fractions:

1. First, students need to understand that the larger the number of parts into which a whole has been divided, the more parts you need for the same amount of the whole.

2. Later, this generalization can be extended to the proportional relationship between the number of parts in the whole and the number of parts required. If there are twice as many parts for the same whole, then you need twice as many of them for the same amount of whatever is being divided.

Randy and Megan each had the same chocolate bar. Randy broke hers into four pieces and ate two of them. Megan broke hers into two half pieces and ate one half. Did they eat the same or different amounts of candy? Explain your answer.

Randy ate _____ of a candy bar.

Megan ate _____ of a candy bar.

_____ = _____ of a candy bar.

Luis and his three friends went for pizza. They ordered a large pie and divided it equally into four pieces. Angelo came in with seven friends and they ordered two large pizzas. They divided each pie into eight parts and each of them had two pieces. Angelo bragged that he had more pizza than Luis. Is he right? Explain your answer. Suppose Angelo had shared the two pizzas among six friends. Would two pieces be the same as Luis's one piece? Use your fraction parts to help you think of other compare-fraction problems in the pizza parlor.

ONE WHOLE LARGE PIE							
½				½			
¼		¼		¼		¼	
1/8	1/8	1/8	1/8	1/8	1/8	1/8	1/8
1/3		1/3		1/3			
1/6		1/6		1/6		1/6	

71 Several approaches can be used to demonstrate the patterns that lead to the generalization that the value of a fraction does not change if numerator and denominator are multiplied or divided by the same quantity. Use real problems such as the ones in on this page and the previous page. Allow the students to see the relationships between fraction bars, egg cartons, and tables of equivalent fractions.

Jenny and Inge had equal numbers of pages in their notebooks. Jenny had hers divided into eight sections, and Inge had hers divided into four sections. What part of the whole was each of Jenny's sections? What part of the whole was each of Inge's? They each counted the number of pages in two sections of their notebooks. Which one had more pages? Whose sections were smaller parts of the whole? How many of Jenny's sections would be the same as two of Inge's? How many of Inge's would be the same as six of Jenny's? Jennie had her book divided into _____ as many parts of the whole as Inge, so she needed _____ as many of these parts to equal Inge's.

Then move to the symbolic algorithm for finding equivalents: that multiplying or dividing the numerator and denominator by the same *operator* forms an equivalent fraction.

The fraction that describes two of Inge's sections is ²⁄₄, and the one that describes four of Jenny's sections is ⁴⁄₈. We found that these were equal: ²⁄₄ = ⁴⁄₈. Look at the two numerators and then look at the two denominators. Do you see a pattern? Can you find another fraction that follows the same pattern? Use your fraction bars to prove that this fraction is equal to the others.

The concept may be reinforced later with a connection to the concept that a fraction with the same numerator and denominator is equal to 1, and therefore multiplying by such a fraction does not change its value.

Look at the A egg carton. Find the halves. How many eggs are in 1/2 dozen?
1/2 = _____ eggs.
Find the twelfths. How many of these in 1/2 dozen?
1/2 = 6/12 = _____ eggs.

Look at the B egg carton. Find the sixths. How many eggs in 1/6 dozen?
1/6 = _____/12 (how many twelfths).
1/6 = _____/12 = _____ eggs.

Look at the C egg carton. Find the thirds. How many thirds in the whole carton?
How many eggs in one third?
How many twelfths of the whole is that?
How many eggs in two thirds of the whole carton? How many twelfths is that?
1/3 = _____/12 = _____ eggs.
2/3 = _____/12 = _____ eggs.

Look at the D carton. How many eggs? What part of the whole is that?
_____/12 = _____/6 = _____ eggs.

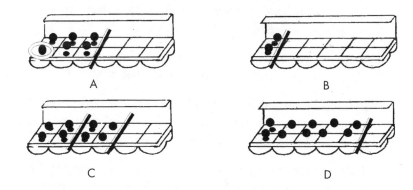

A   B

C   D

All of these fractions represent 1/3 of the whole: 1/3, 2/6, 4/12, 8/24.
Look at the numerators. Do you see a pattern? Look at the denominators. Do you see a pattern? Supply the missing denominator for the next fraction in this series. 16/_____.
Name at least two more fractions that are same as 1/3.
How could you change 3/15 to an equal fraction with five in the denominator?

$$\frac{\bigcirc\bigcirc\bigcirc}{\bigcirc\bigcirc\bigcirc\bigcirc\bigcirc\bigcirc\bigcirc\bigcirc\bigcirc\bigcirc\bigcirc\bigcirc\bigcirc\bigcirc\bigcirc} \quad \begin{array}{c} \div \,? = \\ \div \,? = \end{array} \quad \frac{\bigcirc}{\bigcirc\bigcirc\bigcirc\bigcirc\bigcirc}$$

Three parts out of fifteen are the same as one part out of _____.

72
**
84

I often compare fractions to actors. Actors play different roles with different costumes and settings but underneath are always the same person.

Other generalizations that need to be developed simultaneously involve the concepts of fractions as ratios. As a multiplicative function, ratios and proportions can be considered from the aspect of either (a) comparing multiple units or (b) enlarging and shrinking a single unit. Equivalent fractions can be expressed as ratios. One out of six parts is the same as 2 out of 12. Students can also compare inequalities:

I have 15 video games, and three of them are new. My friend has 12 games, including three new ones. Who has the greatest proportion of new ones?

Analyses of ratio problems should include identification of given quantities in terms of parts and wholes.

In each of the above examples, parts are compared to a given whole. In some ratio problems, only the parts are described, and the whole has to be computed first.

There are three experienced soccer players for every two new ones on the team. The total is (5), and three out of every whole of five players, or ⅗ of the players, are experienced.

In other problems, from the shrinkage or enlargement aspect, only the value of the part size may be given, but expressed as a ratio for the whole. As an example of the first type, the figure opposite shows a scale drawing problem where the value or size of the part is compared as a ratio to a unit of measure in the scale, and the whole has to be measured in its scaled form and its actual size computed as a similar ratio.

There are three experienced soccer players for every two new ones on the team. What are the parts in this ratio? What is the size of the whole? What fraction name tells us what part of the whole are experienced players? Suppose there were 15 players on the team. How many would be experienced? How many would be experienced on a team of 20 players?

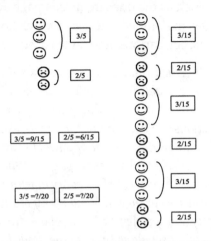

Mavis wanted to know how tall her house was. She couldn't get up to the roof to measure the height, but she had another idea. She took a picture of the house and then measured the height and width of the house on the picture using a centimeter grid. Then she measured the width of the house with a tape measure and found that it was nine meters wide. How could she determine the height of the house from the picture?
Hint: make a scale for the picture using the given measures first.

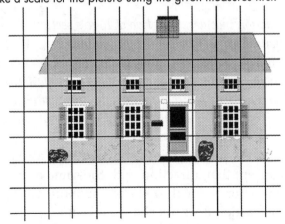

72
**
84
Some ratio problems, such as the one opposite, have no given value for the size of either the whole or the parts— just the relative sizes. Eventually, these ratio problems may be described symbolically as algebraic equations. My size is ⅓ of my father's size ($x = \frac{1}{3}y$). My brother is two times my size ($z = 2x$). My brother is therefore ⅔ of my father's size ($z = \frac{2}{3}y$), and then $y = 1\text{-}\frac{1}{3}z$.

Jim's father is three times as tall as Jim. How many of Jim's heights are in his father's height? What fraction of his father's height is Jim? Jim's brother is twice as tall as Jim. How many of Jim's heights are in his brother's height? What fraction of Jim's father's height is his brother's height? How much taller than Jim's brother is Jim's father?

Jim's height = _____ of his father's height.
Jim's brother's height = _____ × Jim's height.
Jim's brother's height = _____ of his father's height.
Jim's father is _____ times taller than Jim's brother.

73
Fractional inequalities should be explored in several ways in addition to finding the least common denominator (LCD). Begin with inequalities that compare fractions to one whole.

Is ⁹⁄₈ more or less than a whole? Is ⁹⁄₁₀ more or less? Explain why ⁹⁄₈ is more than ⁹⁄₁₀.

After students have developed familiarity with the common equivalents of ½ and realize that any fraction where the denominator is twice the numerator will be equal to ½, inequalities can be solved by comparisons to ½. Is ⅝ smaller or larger than ⁸⁄₁₇? Five ninths is more than ½, and ⁸⁄₁₇ is less than a half (there are alternative ways to reason this), so ⅝ is more than ⁸⁄₁₇.

The cheese pizza pies came sliced into eight pieces and you received seven pieces. How much of a whole cheese pizza is seven pieces? The same size pepperoni pizza came sliced into six pieces and you received seven pieces. Did you get the same amount of pizza?

Finish this number sentence to describe your answer: 7/6 > _____

Which would be more: nine pieces of cheese or seven pieces of pepperoni?

Write the number sentence that describes your answer.

   ▶

75
**
80
An understanding of multiples and factors should precede the introduction of complex operations with fractions. The concept of the associative principle of multiplication is a first step. Let students explore this with arrays of color tiles and balloon diagrams, or with computer drawing programs. When they realize that enlarging a value three times and then two times results in the same outcome as multiplying it six times or the product of the separate increments, you can introduce the concept of common multiple as it relates to the principle.

Beginning, as in the cheese pizza problem on the prevous page, with the value of (3) and multiplying it five times and then multiplying the product of 15 two times is the same as multiplying the original three 2 times and then the product of six five times, and the same as multiplying the original (3) 10 (2 × 5) times.

Ask students to discover other ways to reach a multiple of 30. Use rearrangements of the color tiles to show the result of 30 as a common multiple of 5, 3, 2, and 6, as well as 10, 30, and 1. This list made up of the possible operators (number of repeated units) and the size of the unit to reach 30 are the factors of 30. Each combination of repeated units for the same multiple can be represented by a different rectangle.

Use rectangles made from color tiles to construct other multiples and define the factors. Let students discover that some multiples can have only two factors—the multiple and one—and therefore form only one kind of rectangle, with one side = 1. *These are prime numbers.*

Next, use the tiles to find the smallest possible rectangle that is a multiple of two factors. The rectangle must be capable of being organized into equal-sized arrays of both factors. Each side of the rectangle will be a factor.

The number of tiles in this rectangle is then the least common multiple for two factors.

Blowing up a balloon to two times the size and then making the new size balloon three times bigger is the same as blowing up the original six times.

$$2 \times \bigcirc \times 3 = 6 \times \bigcirc$$

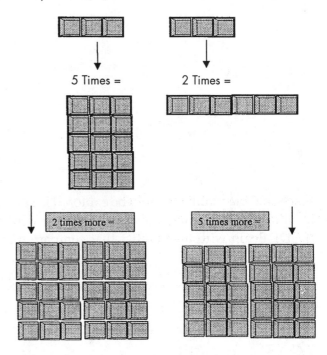

Build these with your color tiles.

Match each equation with a picture and your tiles.
5 × 3 = 15   2 × 3 = 6
2 × 15 = 30   5 × 6 = 30
                10 × 3 = 30
                1 × 30 = 30

30 is a common multiple of 5, _____, _____, _____, _____, _____, _____, and _____.

82 The common relationships between factors and their multiples can be explored with tiles and then organized into tables. Some multiples have common factors. There are whole groups of 12, 6, 4, 3, 2, and 1 in 12 and 24. They are common factors of the different multiples 12 and 24. A balloon of size 12 can shrink three whole times to size 4, four whole times to size 3, or six whole times to size 2. A balloon of size 24 can shrink six whole times to size 4, two whole times to size 12, or 12 whole times to size 2.

Two and four are also common factors of 8, but three is not, because there is not a whole number of threes in 8. A balloon of size eight can shrink four whole times to size 2 or two whole times to size 4, but it cannot shrink three whole times to a whole number. It is also useful to find the greatest common factor.

Use your color tiles to find all of the factors of 12 and 24. Then, find the factors of eight. Make a table of factors and common factors. Explain any difference.

Multiple	All Factors	Common Factors of 12 and 24	Common Factors of 8 and 12	Common Factors of 8 and 24
12				
24				
8				

For each of the multiples above, circle the greatest common factor.

83 Different factors can have many common multiples, but the least common multiple (LCM) is the one that is the smallest. Let students use color tiles to discover these and the generalization that although for two prime numbers, the (LCM) is the product of the two, other LCMs will be less than the product of the factors.

Use your color tiles to find the least common multiples for these factors. Construct the smallest rectangle that contains whole groups of each factor.

Factors	Least Common Multiple
3, 4, 2, 12	
7, 3, 1	
7, 3, 6, 21	

83   The concept of factors and common factors is critical as a basis for solving complex algebraic equations, and practice will be needed for this. Use the color tiles and tables as in #82, but factor trees can also work. Try relating factors to measures.

Use exchanges in money to make the concept real. A dime and a quarter are common factors of the dollar because you can change the dollar for only dimes or only quarters. But the dime is not a factor of the quarter because the quarter cannot be exchanged for a whole number of dimes. It is a factor of a half-dollar. Nickels and pennies are common factors of the quarter, the dime, and the half-dollar.

84   Construction of the algorithm for finding the LCD and
**   changing fractions to common denominators so that opera-
86   tions can be performed should occur in the context of solving addition and subtraction problems with manipulatives.

Fraction bars work well in developing a purpose for the common denominator and in visualizing what is happening as fractions are operated on. Use scaffolding, such as that in the figures opposite and on the next page, to bring students to the generalization that multiplying numerator and denominator by the same operator does not change the value, and that in order to add or subtract fractions, we need to find the denominators that are common multiples for the fractions on which we wish to operate—preferably the least common multiple. Provide some practice with finding common denominators in just the algorithm form. However, it may be unnecessary to have extensive practice with these once the concepts are clear, because it is much simpler to convert the fractions to decimals by dividing the numerator by the denominator with a calculator and then performing the operation.

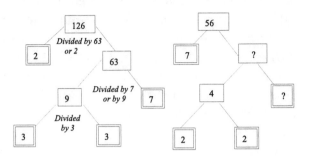

Try building a factor tree. Study the tree for 126 and then try to fill in the missing places in the 56 tree. Explain why there are no branches coming from the double line boxes. Build a tree of your own from a number you choose.

Maria ate 1/4 of a candy bar before lunch and 1/3 of the same kind of candy bar after lunch. How much of a whole candy bar did she eat? Use your fraction tiles to help solve this problem. Add the pieces by putting them together. Do you see an equivalent fraction that is equal to their sum? In order to add the two different fractions we had to change them into fractions that had the same denominator. How can we do that without changing the value of the fraction? Look at the denominators of 1/3 and 1/4. Can you find their **least common multiple?** That will be your **least common denominator.** Now find the numerator for the denominator that makes an equivalent for each fraction. Remember, the numerator has to be enlarged as much as the denominator because the greater the number of parts of a whole, the more parts you need for the same amount.

1/3 = _____/12, 1/4 = _____/12.

Now add them together.

4/12 + 3/12 = _____ and therefore 1/3 + 1/4 = _____

12 is the **least common multiple** of the numbers _____ and _____.

It is also the **least common denominator** of the fractions _____ and _____.

ONE WHOLE					
½			½		
¼	¼		¼		¼
1/3		1/3		1/3	
1/6	1/6	1/6	1/6	1/6	1/6
1/12 1/12 1/12 1/12 1/12 1/12 1/12				1/12 1/12 1/12 1/12 1/12	
1/3		¼			

86
**
90

Practice with both the horizontal and vertical algorithm forms for addition and subtraction of unlike fractions should be attached to real problems. A critical generalization is the recognition that finding the LCD is a first and important step. Relating this to operations with whole numbers and the need to add and subtract like quantities helps. Use the color tiles for discovering the LCD, and then allow students to suggest addition and subtraction algorithm forms, including making a note of the LCD as a reference for converting to equivalents. I suggest not shortcutting the converted full equivalent fraction form by just recording the numerators (a traditional form) at first. This may be disjunctive to the reasoning process. Consider the following sequence of transitions with increasing difficulty.

1. Present only problems with proper fractions and easily computed common multiples (LCDs) that do not add up to more than one whole.

2. Present problems that add up to more than one whole, develop vocabulary for improper fractions and mixed numbers, and practice changing in either direction. Compare the process to trading with whole numbers.

3. Present problems that require finding the difference between proper fractions.

4. Present problems that require finding the difference between improper fractions, but do not require trading.

5. Present subtraction problems with fractions of all types that require trading.

Maria ate 1/4 of a candy bar before lunch and 1/3 of the same kind of candy bar after lunch. Which was the larger piece? How much larger was that piece? Use your fraction tiles to help solve this problem. Compare the fraction pieces. Do you see a fraction that is equal to the difference between the two pieces? It has a different denominator, but the fractions we are comparing have equivalents for that denominator. In order to find the difference between two fractions with different denominators, we have to change them into fractions that have the same, or common, denominator. What was the common denominator in this problem?

1/3 = ____/____   1/4 = ____/____   ____/12 - ____/12 = ____

1/3 - 1/4 = ____.

Steve went trick-or-treating on Halloween. By the end of the evening at 9:00 p.m., he had collected seven of his favorite chocolate bars. He couldn't resist eating them, however, and by 7:00 p.m., one of them was half gone. At 9:00 p.m., he had only 4¾ bars left. How much more candy had he eaten between 7:00 p.m. and 9:00 p.m.?

Think: Altogether Steve collected ☐ bars.

He ate ☐ bars before 7:00 P.M.

That left him with ☐ more bars of candy to eat.
The candy he ate between 7:00 and 9:00 is the difference between ☐ and ☐ .

The number sentence for this is:_____

91 Steve's problem on the preceding page is a complex, multistep problem that represents a change unknown subtraction involving unlike fractions. The algorithm presented by Rhonda varies from the traditional in that the equivalent fractions are shown with both numerator and denominator. Students may then suggest shortcuts and share these.

Rhonda solved Steve's Halloween problem with this algorithm. Explain how she did it.

A	B	C
$6\frac{1}{2}$ →	$6\frac{2}{4}$ →	$5\frac{6}{4}$
$4\frac{3}{4}$	$4\frac{3}{4}$	$4\frac{3}{4}$
		$1\frac{3}{4}$

How did she get from A to B?

How did she get from B to C?

How did she find the difference between $5\frac{6}{4}$ and $4\frac{3}{4}$?

92 Multiplication of proper fractions by whole number operators should be presented as repeated addition of the same fraction. Using manipulatives and real materials, students should discover that, as in the addition of like fractions, the numerators are enlarged but the denominators remain the same. In other words, 1/3 repeated two whole times is 2/3, and 2/5 repeated three times is 6/5.

Allow students to discover that just the numerators have to be multiplied, whereas the denominators remain the same, before moving to the horizontal and vertical algorithm. Follow this with multiplication of mixed numbers by whole numbers—changing to improper fractions.

The running track on which Lori ran was $1\frac{1}{2}$ miles long. How many miles did she run in three laps? Try this problem, but estimate your answer first.

Allan tried to solve the running track problem with an algorithm. Explain how he got from A to B, from B to C, and then to D.

A	B	C	D
$3 \times 1\frac{1}{2}$ =	$3 \times \frac{3}{2}$ =	$\frac{9}{2}$ =	$4\frac{1}{2}$

Did you find the same answer in a different way? Explain it to your group.

93   Multiplying by a fractional operator is a difficult but important concept. At the beginning, students need to discover that multiplication by a fractional operator is the same as repeating the referent value less than one whole time; therefore, the product or result will have a value less than the referent. It is also the same as finding the fractional part of a value. If the operator is a unit fraction, it is the same as dividing the value by the denominator. ½ times 24 is the same as ½ of 24 and the same as dividing 24 by 2. ½ × 24 = ½ of 24 = 24 ÷ 2.

Every time the small hand of a clock goes around one whole time, 12 hours pass. Two times around covers ? hours, but ½ time around is only ½ of the twelve or ? hours. Football games also play by the clock. The total playing time is 1 hour. How much time is used up at halftime?

93   The next step is to consider more-than-unit fractions of whole
**   number values. Begin to develop the algorithm for multi-
94   plication of fractions with students by generalizing back to back the concept that two times ⅓ is ⅔, and thus ⅔ of a value is two times more than whatever ⅓ of that value is.

Once you find ⅓, then you just have to multiply the numerator by 2 in order to find ⅔.

By using the fraction tiles and referring back to the above, students can apply their generalizations to multiplication operations on fractions. Multiplying a fraction by a proper fraction operator is like finding a fractional part of the referent fraction, and the resulting product is going to be less than the referent fraction. Extend this with number sense analysis. The student can easily see that ½ × ⅓ is going to be ⅙ , and ⅓ of ½ is going to be the same ⅙ , and that ½ of ⅙ is ¹⁄₁₂. The generalization can then be made that this result of the operation can be obtained by multiplying the denominators of the operator and the referent value—in effect, producing a fraction with a larger denominator and smaller value.

For each of the following number sentences, estimate whether the answer will be more or less than the value in the box.

$$\tfrac{1}{3} \times \boxed{4} = ? \qquad 1\tfrac{1}{3} \times \boxed{4} = ?$$

Then, try the multiplication algorithm to find the answer.

One day Lori fell when she was only halfway around the 1½-mile track. How far did she run? She made up for it the next day by running 5½ times around the track. How far did she run that day?

  ▶

94 Review the concept above that finding a more-than-a-unit fraction of a whole number requires us to multiply the value of a unit fraction of the number by the numerator of the operator ($\frac{3}{2}$ of 6 is equal to $3 \times \frac{1}{2}$ of 6 or three times greater than $\frac{1}{2} \times 6$).

Then consider more-than-a-unit fraction of a *fraction*. Referring to the hike problem: $3 \times (\frac{1}{2}$ of $\frac{1}{3})$ is the same as $\frac{3}{2}$ of $\frac{1}{3}$ *and also the same as* $\frac{3}{2} \times \frac{1}{3}$.

It follows that if $\frac{1}{2} \times \frac{1}{3} = \frac{1}{6}$ (multiplying denominators), then $\frac{3}{2} \times \frac{1}{3}$ is 3 times greater or equal to $\frac{3}{6}$ (multiplying numerators as well). These combined concepts construct the algorithm.

Prove the algorithm with fraction tiles. Prove the algorithm again with number sense operations. $\frac{1}{2} \times \frac{2}{3} = \frac{1}{3}$ because it is $\frac{2}{3}$ only a half a time. $\frac{1}{5} \times \frac{5}{6} = \frac{1}{6}$ because it is $\frac{5}{6}$ only $\frac{1}{5}$ of a time.

95 The process of reducing a fraction to lowest terms has some function in making work with fractions simpler and is useful in understanding ratios. However, with calculators in everyday use, most complex fraction operations should be done by translating the fraction to a decimal. In solving a problem, the unreduced fraction is not a wrong answer unless the problem specifically says: reduce to lowest terms. Refer back to understandings of equivalent fractions, ratios, and factors to help students generalize:

1. That dividing numerator and denominator by the same factor does not change the value of a fraction

2. That dividing numerator and denominator by their greatest common factor will reduce the fraction to lowest terms

---

Mike and Dan were on a hike. They filled up their 1/3-gallon jug with water at every spring and shared the water equally. How much water did each boy drink by the time they filled and emptied the jug three times?
Use your fraction tiles to solve this problem.
Hint: First find out how much water each friend drank from each refill.
Mike and Dan each drank _____ of 1/3 of a gallon of water from each refill. This is the same as _____ of a gallon for each refill.
By the end of the hike, they had each consumed 3 times _____ of a gallon.
Counting all three refills, they each drank _____ of a gallon.
The number sentence for this problem is: $3 \times (1/2 \text{ of } 1/3) =$ _____.
Think about what you did to solve the problem and think of a simple way to explain how to do it from the number sentence. There may be more than one way to solve the problem.

It rains in parts of Arizona an average of 15 days a year. We were in Arizona for 75 days, and it rained on three of them. Was that close to average?

1. Express the ratio of average rainfall as a fraction.

2. How can we make the denominator of this fraction closer to 75 (our number of days) without changing the value of the fraction?

3. Explain your answer and how you found it.

96 Use fraction bars or tiles to help concept development of division of fractions by whole numbers from the partitive view in this sequence:

1. Begin with unit fractions and a review of the concept that the value of unit fractions decreases proportionately with the size of the denominator. $\frac{1}{3}$ divided into 2 parts is $\frac{1}{6}$.

2. Follow with more than unit fractions with the same denominator and numerators that can be divided evenly.

3. Students can then discover that when the numerator cannot be divided evenly by the divisor, you can change the fraction to smaller sized equivalents and divide these.

4. Refer back to the concept that dividing a value into parts is the same as finding that unit fraction of it; $\frac{1}{6} \div 5$ is the same as $\frac{1}{5}$ of $\frac{1}{6}$ and $\frac{1}{5} \times \frac{1}{6}$.

5. Connect this to the concept that whole numbers can be represented by fractions with the denominator of 1, and this may lead to the "invert and multiply" algorithm generalization. Practice the transfer to multiplication using problems with proper and improper fractions as well as mixed numbers.

Roger and Dean bought a large bag of chips to eat at the football game. They had eaten about half of it when they were joined by Brad at the halftime break. They then shared the rest of the bag among the three of them. What fraction of a whole bag of chips did they each have after the break? Use your fraction bars to help.

1. What did the boys have to do with the $\frac{1}{2}$ bag?

2. Complete the number sentence for their problem: $\frac{1}{2} \div$ ___ = ___

3. That is the same as finding $1/$ ___ of $\frac{1}{2}$.

Finding a fractional part of a value is the same as multiplying by the fraction.

4. Then $\frac{1}{3}$ of $\frac{1}{2}$ is the same as $\frac{1}{3} \times \frac{1}{2}$, and that is also the same as $\frac{1}{2} \times$?; and the same as $\frac{1}{2} \div 3$.

5. Explain why we can think of three wholes as $\frac{3}{1}$.

6. Then $\frac{1}{2} \div 3$ is the same as $\frac{1}{2} \div \frac{3}{1}$.

But in #4 above, we learned that $\frac{1}{2} \div \frac{3}{1} = \frac{1}{2} \times \frac{1}{3}$.

Can you recognize an algorithm or shortcut procedure for dividing a fraction?

Try the algorithm on this number sentence: $\frac{5}{6} \div 5 =$ ___ Explain how you used the algorithm to solve this. Use your number sense to verify that your answer was correct.

If you divided $\frac{5}{6}$ of a pizza pie among five friends, how much of a pie would each one get?

96 Division of fractions by whole numbers from the quotitive view is more challenging but requires attention for its number sense impact. The quantity of any whole value in a fraction that is less than a whole is going to be less than the whole. There is less than one group of three in ½. There is only ⅙ of a group of three in ½.

Division of a value by a fractional divisor is a difficult-to-understand concept. It is frequently confused with finding a fractional part of the value. The first clarification, then, has to relate back to the meaning of division. The partition meaning of division does not work for division *by* a fraction because a fraction is not a counting number. You can divide a value into two parts or one part, but you cannot divide a value into ½ number of parts. The quotition meaning works. You can divide a value into parts that are of a size that is ½ of one whole. When we divide 4 by ½, we think: "How many parts of size ½ of one whole are there in 4?"

Reggie took the same vitamin pills each morning. The pills came in a box, and each day he took two pills. One day he noticed that the box was close to empty. He counted the pills and figured out how long they would last if he continued to take two pills each day. How many days would the pills last? Reggie then decided that he would need to stretch the pills by taking one pill each day instead. Now how many days would they last? How many days would they last if he only took half a pill each day? What fractional part of the normal dose would half a pill be?

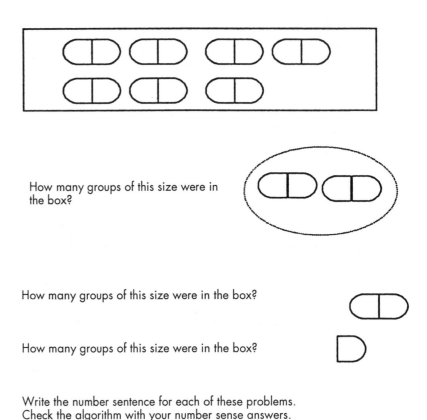

How many groups of this size were in the box?

How many groups of this size were in the box?

How many groups of this size were in the box?

Write the number sentence for each of these problems. Check the algorithm with your number sense answers.

Solomon, P. *The Math We Need to "Know" and "Do": Content Standards for Elementary and Middle Grades.* © 2001. Corwin Press, Inc.

97
**
98

Once there is clarity in the concept of what is happening in the division of a value by a fraction, there is still the challenge of developing a true understanding of the algorithm for division by a fraction. Step-by-step interpretations of problems such as those illustrated that describe real situations will help. Then try to develop the following sequence of concepts:

1. Start with division of whole values by a unit fraction. The number of unit fractions in any one whole is the same as the denominator of a fraction. One whole = $\frac{4}{4}$. Two wholes would have twice as many units or $2 \times$ the denominator or $\frac{8}{4}$. The generalization here is that to find the number of unit fractions in values of more than one whole, we just multiply the whole number which is the dividend by the denominator of the divisor. $6 \div \frac{1}{4} = 24$ because there are four unit fractions of size $\frac{1}{4}$ in one whole and 6 times as many (6×4) $\frac{1}{4}^{\text{ths}}$ in six wholes.

2. Then proceed to mixed-number dividends and more-than-unit fraction divisors. The problem $6 \div \frac{2}{4}$ means: "How many $\frac{2}{4}^{\text{ths}}$ are there in 6?" Although there are four unit fractions ($\frac{1}{4}^{\text{ths}}$) in one whole, there are only half as many $\frac{2}{4}^{\text{ths}}$. There are only half as many because $\frac{2}{4}$ is twice as large as $\frac{1}{4}$. There would also be only $\frac{1}{3}$ as many $\frac{3}{4}^{\text{ths}}$ in the same whole.

If there are (24) $\frac{1}{4}^{\text{ths}}$ in 6, then there are only (12) $\frac{2}{4}^{\text{ths}}$ and only (8) $\frac{3}{4}^{\text{ths}}$. In each case, we found the number of more-than-unit fractions in the dividend (6) by dividing the number of unit fractions in the dividend (24) by the numerator of the divisor: 2 or 3.

Jenna wanted to make some banners for the cheering squad. She went to the material store and bought five yards of material. Each banner needed $\frac{1}{3}$ of a yard. How many banners could she make? Use your fraction tiles or a diagram to help.

Write a number sentence for this problem. Think of the following: How many banners could she make with one yard, or how many $\frac{1}{3}$ yards are there in one whole yard? How many in 5 yards?

Jenna tried to find an algorithm to solve the material problem of dividing 5 by $\frac{1}{3}$. First, she thought about the problem as "How many $\frac{1}{3}$ yards are there in 5 yards?" Then, she listed the three steps she needed to solve the problem: A, B, and C. Explain what she did in each step. Why did she do Step B? Why did she do Step C?

A. 5 yds $\div \frac{1}{3}$ yd = ? banners
B. 1 yard = 3 banners
C. 5 × 3 banners = 15 banners

Then, she decided that $5 \div \frac{1}{3}$ was the same as $5 \times \frac{3}{1}$. Do you agree?

Suppose she had bought 8 yards. How many banners could she make? Solve the problem in your head, and then try Jenna's algorithm to see if it works.

Solomon, P. *The Math We Need to "Know" and "Do": Content Standards for Elementary and Middle Grades.* © 2001. Corwin Press, Inc.   ▶

97
**
98
The generalization to aim for is that dividing the total number of unit fractions in a given dividend by the numerator of a more-than-unit fraction divisor then tells us the number of more-than-unit fractions there are in the dividend.

The algorithm combines the two concepts: multiply the dividend by the denominator of the divisor to find the number of unit fractions in the dividend, and then divide by the numerator of the divisor to find the number of more-than-unit fractions in it—or just invert the divisor and multiply by it.

99 Construction of the meaning of decimals can begin with an understanding of the common notations for money. Children will learn these notations as alternate number names without complete constructs of what decimals are. Their cultural experience with money and intrinsic motivation to communicate about it will encourage the process.

Then try Jenna's problem with $6\frac{1}{3}$ yards. You will have to change the mixed number to an improper fraction first.

$6\frac{1}{3}$ yards ÷ $\frac{1}{3}$ yard = ?

Suppose Jenna wanted to make double-sized banners. She would need $\frac{2}{3}$ yard for each. How many can she make from 6 yards of material? Try using Jenna's algorithm.

Write the decimal number symbols for the amount of money each of these is worth under each picture.

100 Decimal concepts can be constructed with two parallel connections to prior knowledge: place value and fractions. These connections should be presented as parallel to each other in problem applications that involve decimals. Decimals are, in effect, a way of making fractions fit our number system—an extension of our number notation system to include values that are less than one whole, but they are therefore also fractions. They are special fractions in multiples of 10 or decimal fractions. Early concepts developed for money can be expanded to develop further understanding, but base 10 blocks are also useful. Before they can be used, however, students will have to make a transition from the understanding of their application as whole number representations to decimal representations. This will need careful scaffolding. The flat that represented 100 ones now becomes one whole or 100 hundredths. The rod or stick becomes one tenth of the whole or 10 one hundredths, and the unit cube becomes one one hundredth of the whole.

Relate the reality (money) and the manipulative representations (base 10 blocks) to each other and then to their number system place-value relationships in a triad that also includes the descriptive words and the symbolic form. When using words, avoid the use of the term *point* to mark the decimal point terminus for whole numbers. Instead, use the word "and" (e.g., five and two tenths) as though it were a whole number and fraction (which it is). This forces some meaning into the words that are missing when the value is just read as digits after the decimal. Students should discover that the need for zero as a place holder is opposite that for a whole number, where a zero is not needed for values larger than the largest digit value. For decimals, it is not needed for values less than the smallest digit value. We do not need zeros at either end, but we need them for all of the empty places in between.

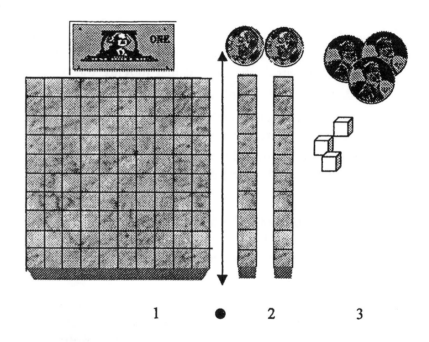

1   ●   2   3

Make the trades with your blocks and money.

One whole + 2 tenths + 3 hundredths

= _____ tenths + 3 hundredths

= _____ hundredths

101 Compare values of decimals using sequences of values in
** both the decimal and common fraction form.
103

Use your base 10 blocks to help put the following values in order from the smallest to the largest: $\frac{1}{10}$, .09, .2, $\frac{1}{100}$.

Compare decimals as multiples of each other. One tenth (.1) is 10 times as much as (?). One whole is 100 times as large as ?

Use a left and right shift of place value (see #14) to enlarge and shrink decimals by multiples of 10. Check with a calculator. If students suggest just moving the decimal point, ask them to explain why this works.

Use base 10 blocks and money to rename and trade decimals: .12 is 12 one hundredths, but it is also one tenth and two one hundredths or a dime and two pennies. The number 1.12 is 112 one hundredths or one dollar and 12 cents.

Use base 10 blocks and money to identify .5 as half of one whole and .05 as half of one tenth. Then, round decimals to the nearest whole or tenth.

104 Because decimals are an extension of our number system, addition and subtraction operations with decimals can be handled in the same way as whole number multiples of 10. Only like things can be added and subtracted, and when we have too many of one kind to fit into our system or not enough—we trade. Start with money, and then use other real data that are reported in decimal form, such as rainfall amounts and batting averages. Compare decimal data by making graphs and using spreadsheet computer programs to translate data lists into graphic representations. Get data from the Internet.

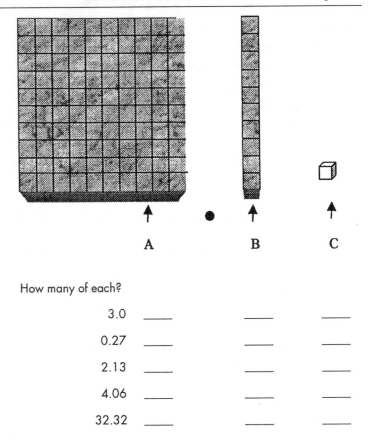

A   B   C

How many of each?

	A	B	C
3.0	____	____	____
0.27	____	____	____
2.13	____	____	____
4.06	____	____	____
32.32	____	____	____

The least average yearly rainfall in the world is recorded in Arica, Chile. It is only .03 of an inch. The least annual average rainfall in the United States is recorded at Death Valley, California. It is 1.63 inches. What is the difference between the average annual rainfall in these desert communities? The average annual rainfall for the entire world is about 34 inches. How much more is that than the rainfall in Death Valley? The most rainfall in the United States occurs in the Pacific Northwest, where they get about 100 inches. Find the difference in average annual rainfall between the most and least rainy places in the United States.

105 Begin developing concepts related to multiplication by deci-
**   mals with decimal values of wholes. The first generaliza-
106 tion is that multiplying by a decimal fraction (as recalled
from common fractions) is the same as finding a fractional
part of it. .5 times a value is the same as $\frac{5}{10}$ or $\frac{1}{2}$ of the
value. Area problems can help students visualize varying
sized wholes and their decimal or common fraction equal
parts. Another important generalization to recall from
fractions at this time is that the size of the parts depends
upon the size of the whole. .5 of 70 is not the same as .5 of
80.

Alternating between the decimal and common fraction
should help students emerge with the next generalization—that when multiplying by a decimal, just as it is in
multiplication by fractions, we multiply by the numerator
and divide by the denominator to find the fractional
value. One possible thinking sequence follows:

1. If we are multiplying the whole number value (5) by
   .6, which is the same as finding $\frac{6}{10}$ of it, we multiply
   the 5 by the numerator of 6 and divide by the denominator of 10. $6 \times 5 = 30$, but for $.6 \times 5$ we have to divide
   the 30 by 10 to get a quotient of 3. We can use the
   shortcut of a right shift to do this.

2. This leads to the shortcut of just multiplying by the
   decimal digit and then dividing the product by the
   place value of the digit, which is the denominator of
   the corresponding common fraction. As an example,
   $.06 \times 5$ would be .30 because the digit 6 in this place
   represents $\frac{6}{100}$. The product is then $\frac{30}{100}$ or, in decimal
   form, .30.

Steven wanted to plant a garden. He marked off a plot that was six meters
by eight meters. What was the area of his plot? He wanted to carefully lay
out parts of the garden and constructed a wire grid to help. He first divided it
into two equal halves. What common fraction and decimal fraction would
represent half of the plot? How much area would that be? How did you find
your answer?

Steven then decided that he would like to grow vegetables in a little more
than half of his garden. He used more wire to divide his garden into 100
equal parts. The part for vegetables is shaded on the picture below. What
decimal fraction of the whole garden plot does this represent? Can you
rename the decimal in an easier form? How much of the whole area would
be vegetables? Explain how you found your answer.

Steven also wanted some herbs and decided to plant just .04 of the plot with
herbs. Shade the part that would be herbs. What would be the area of the
herb portion of the garden?

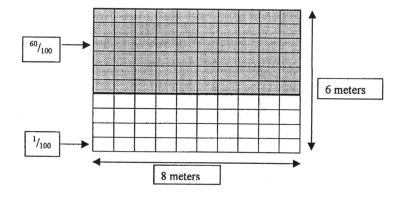

▶

107 Once the generalization for multiplication by a decimal is in place (multiplying by the digit and dividing the product by the denominator of its place value), students can quickly progress to more-than-single-digit decimal multipliers. They will realize that they can proceed with the partial products and trading as though they were dealing with whole numbers. Then, for the final result, they will need to divide by the place value of the operator or multiplier (the same as the denominator of its corresponding common fraction). This can be done with a simple right shift past the decimal point. Some students will suggest the counting of decimal places for this. Teachers should get them to explain why this works.

The next step is understanding what happens when both the multiplicand and the multiplier are decimals. Revert back again to the multiplication of common fractions to demonstrate that multiplying tenths times tenths will result in hundredths as the denominators are multiplied. This should lead to the realization that in the algorithm, multiplying $.6 \times .6$ will result in .36 and needs to be so recorded in the partial product. However, the counting decimal places shortcut works here as well.

Extend the concept to the following: *tenths times hundredths are thousandths, and therefore, $.06 \times .6$ is .036 or $2 + 1 = 3$ decimal places.*

The smallest place value in the product will be the result of multiplying the denominators of the two smallest decimal digits. Sometimes, the product of the digits (numerators) will be a multiple of 10, and then, because it is a decimal, we reduce to lowest terms. $.6 \times .5 = .30$, but $\frac{30}{100}$ is the same as $\frac{3}{10}$. Therefore, in decimal form, we ignore zeros to the right of the smallest place value that has a nonzero digit.

The average annual rainfall in the northwestern United States is 99.7 inches. How much rain would fall (on the average) in 3.3 years?

1. Round the rainfall data to the nearest whole number.

2. Estimate your answer in whole numbers.

3. Predict how many decimal places there will be in the exact answer.

4. Compute an exact answer using the multiplication algorithm.

5. Explain how the algorithm worked to get you an exact answer. Does it agree with your estimate?

108 Because the percentage application of decimals is in such
** common use in our culture, it may be wise to approach
109 percent problems in tandem with multiplication by decimals. Finding the percent of a number and describing change in terms of percent is the everyday application of this operation—usually with the decimal rounded off to the nearest hundredth as the percent sign takes the place of the decimal point.

The development of number sense in the application of percent concepts may be one of the most important preparations for full participation in the mathematical communications of our present culture. Spatial perceptions of objects accompanied by quantitative descriptions in both percent and common fraction form will help students achieve the necessary concepts. Students should be able to mentally visualize and estimate how large 50%, 25%, 33⅓%, 75%, and 10% of an object is. Connections to the corresponding common fractions in lowest terms for these should be computed and then automatized.

Using their previously developed fraction and decimal concepts, students should be encouraged to try alternative approaches to finding commonly used percent values, including the following:

▷ Dividing the value by 2 (finding ½) for 50%

▷ Dividing the value by 4 for 25% (finding ¼) and then multiplying by 3 (finding ¾) for 75%

▷ Dividing by 3 for 33⅓% (finding ⅓)

▷ Right shifting one place for 10% and two places for 1%

▷ Doubling the result of a one-place right shift for 20%

▷ Adding half of 10% to 10% to compute a 15% tip

Another important functional skill in problem solving with percentages is the language distinction between 20% off and 20% of a value. Ask the following scaffolding question: What part of the whole are you looking for when you take 20% off?

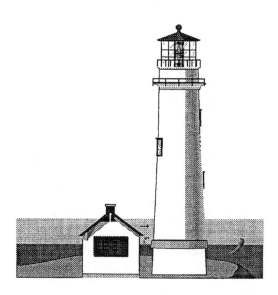

Compare the pictures of the home and the lighthouse. About what percentage of the height of the lighthouse is the height of the home? Choose from 33%, 50%, 10%, or 75%.

Draw another house that is ¾ the size of the lighthouse. What percentage of the lighthouse would that be?

108 *Explain the difference between 20% of and 20% off. Twenty*
** *percent off a value is the same as what percent of the value?*
109

Another data analysis and cultural survival skill is the realization that sequential percentage diminutions or accretions of a value are not additive. Taking 50% off of a value and then taking off 20% more is not the same as taking 70% off the original. The concept to connect back to is that the value of fractional parts depends upon the size of the whole. The larger the whole, the larger the value of the percentage or decimal fraction. After you shrink a value by 50%, 20% of the result is less than 20% of the original value.

This concept has other applications besides department store sales. If the crime rate goes down an even 10% per year, the actual decrease in the number of crimes gets smaller each year. On the other end, if you measured your growth over a 5-year period and discovered that you grew an even 10% per year, when did you grow the most?

110 Division of decimal values by whole numbers can be explained both from a partitive and quotitive view like division of the corresponding fraction—just dividing the numerator and maintaining the same denominator. For example, .6 of a candy bar divided into three parts is equal to .2 of a candy bar.

As in the division of common fractions, an important concept is that we can exchange fractions for their smaller size equivalents so that division is possible. The concept of trading whole numbers for their smaller sized decimal equivalents for the purpose of dividing them can then be applied to the traditional division algorithm form. Use base 10 blocks to help develop this concept, translating the manipulative to the symbolic decimal form step by step.

Evan kept a record of how much he grew each year. He showed it to his friends and said that he grew 5% each year. He always rounded his new height to the nearest inch. His friends said that he was wrong because he did not grow the same amount each year. Who is right, Evan or his friends? Explain your answer. If Evan continued growing at the same rate, will he ever grow five inches in one year? Predict when that would happen. Is it likely to happen? Can you find a pattern for his increase in size?

Year	Height	Percent Change
1	46 in	
2	48 in	5
3	50 in	5
4	53 in	5
5	56 in	5
6	59 in	5
7	62 in	5
8	65 in	5
9	68 in	5
10	71 in	5
11	75 in	5

Cindy had to share her three tenths of a package of paper among five friends. She knew she could not divide 3/10 into five equal parts. How could she change the three tenths into smaller parts to divide equally? Explain what she can do with your base 10 blocks.

You just learned that .3 ÷ 5 is the same as ☐ ÷ 5.

The quotient for .30 ÷ 5 = ☐.

If we divide 30 hundredths into equal parts, the quotient will be ☐ hundredths. If we divide .3 into equal parts, the quotient will be ☐. What part of the package will each friend get?
Explain your answer.
How can Cindy find out how many sheets to give each friend?

110 A practical and useful application of the algorithm for division of a decimal is the conversion of any fraction to its decimal form through the process of dividing numerator by denominator and trading indivisible digits and remainders for their smaller sized decimal equivalents.

Clarity in this application requires a review of the concept that any fraction represents the division operation. $\frac{24}{6}$ is the same as 24 wholes ÷ 6 parts. They are both equal to four wholes. However, if you divide six wholes into 10 parts, the number of wholes to be divided is less than the number of parts. The result of this is that the size of each part will be less than one whole or $\frac{6}{10}$ of one whole or, in its decimal form, .6 (see #70).

For operations with fractions whose denominators are not in multiples of 10 and easily translated to decimal form, we can convert them to decimal form by dividing the numerator by the denominator. The calculator does this automatically. Using a calculator for the division process makes converting complex fractions to their decimal equivalents an alternative and easier way of handling complex fraction problems. Instead of converting complex fractions to varying common denominators for the purpose of operations, we can convert them to decimals (which are common denominators with easily traded and operated on multiples of 10).

Denise got a $5 allowance that she wanted to spend equally over 6 days. What fraction of the allowance can she use each day?

$\frac{5}{6}$ is the same as ___ ÷ ___ .

How can she divide a smaller number by a larger number?

1. As a first step, we can change the 5 whole ones into a decimal fraction.

2. What are the tenths and hundredths decimal fraction equivalents for 5 ones? 5 = ? tenths, 5 = ? hundredths.

3. Can you divide these equivalents by 6? Where would you start?

4. Trade 5 whole ones for tenths with your blocks and show what you do in symbolic form with the division algorithm.

5. If you divide the 50 tenths into six parts, the first partial quotient is ___ tenths or (.8). This would use up ___ tenths equally divided into six parts. But we still have a remainder of ___ .

6. Can we trade this remainder for an equivalent decimal with a smaller denominator that we can divide?

7. After we divide the equivalent, what is the next partial quotient? Is there a remainder?

8. Can we trade this for an equivalent decimal with a smaller denominator that we can divide?

9. Explain how you got your final quotient.

111 The process of dividing a decimal by a decimal is again made more meaningful when approached from the common fraction point of view. From the quotitive view, for divisors that are smaller than the dividend, and where the dividend can be equally divided, number sense reveals the concept. The number of $\frac{2}{10}$ in $\frac{6}{10}$ is the same as the number of 2s in 6. There are three whole (.2) in (.6). Then .6/.2 or (.6 ÷ .2) is easily interpreted as the same as (6 ÷ 2). Use the base 10 blocks to help students see this.

For larger divisors, .6 ÷ .7 is the same as .6/.7 or $\frac{6}{10}$/$\frac{7}{10}$. We can change the fractional numerator and denominator to whole numbers by multiplying each by 10 and end up with $\frac{6}{7}$ or 6 ÷ 7, and then proceed with the division algorithm as above.

In the algorithm, we change the decimal divisor (which is the denominator) to a whole number by multiplying it and the dividend (which is the numerator) by the same multiple of 10. If the denominator of the divisor is in the hundredths, then we multiply it and the dividend by 100.

A difficulty that sometimes arises with this process in applying it to problem solving is in interpreting any remainder. In the problem opposite, the algorithm finds the number of .75 (of a whole dollar) in 10 dollars by finding the corresponding number of 75 (dollars) in 1,000 dollars. The answer to the problem is that there are 13 (.75 of a dollar) in 10.00, not 13 groups of 75 whole dollars. And the remainder is not 25 whole dollars, but .25 or 25 cents. When applying the algorithm to problem solving, therefore, it may be a good idea to label the quotient and remainders carefully. They must also make sense. The remainder in the problem is .25 or $\frac{1}{3}$ of .75, but you cannot buy $\frac{1}{3}$ of a token.

Serena has a $10.00 bill to buy some subway tokens. Each token cost 75 cents ($0.75). How many tokens can she get with her $10.00? How much change will she get? Estimate your answer and then try the division algorithm.

1. Explain how to get from A to B.

2. Explain the steps in C.

3. Explain what the remainder in C means.

$$
\begin{array}{lll}
\text{A} & \text{B} & \text{C} \\
 & & \phantom{75\overline{)}}13 \\
.75\,\overline{)10.00} \longrightarrow & 75\,\overline{)1000} & 75\,\overline{)1000} \\
 & & \phantom{75\overline{)1}}\underline{75} \\
 & & \phantom{75\overline{)}}25\,0 \\
 & & \phantom{75\overline{)}}\underline{225} \\
 & & \phantom{75\overline{)1}}25
\end{array}
$$

112
**
155

"The Measurement Magic Dozen"

Measures are the most common application in the study of numbers and operations and should be integrated within the problems presented to develop skill in these. Because of the discrepancy in the standards, students need to learn to estimate and measure in both metrics and English (customary) standard units.

Useful estimates of conversions, such as the quart/liter/gallon, inch/centimeter, mile/kilometer, and foot/meter should be automatized, but use the calculator for the exact conversions.

There are at least 12 general concepts that cut across the various categories of measures. As teachers engage students in problem-solving opportunities to develop knowledge and skill in the more specific parameters of each separate category of measure, they should reinforce these often overlooked concepts.

1. Measures are the descriptive terms for the quantitative properties or attributes of objects and the way they move through space and time.

2. Measures allow us to communicate with each other about these properties and keep records of them.

3. An important use for measures is that they help us use what we know to tell us about what we do not know. For example, we can measure the area of a rectangle by measuring its length and width. We can tell how far a car will travel in an hour at the same speed if we measure the distance it travels in five minutes.

4. In order to communicate with each other about quantitative properties, we have to share or have a common meaning for the descriptive units of measure.

Greg had a friend who lived in another state. They corresponded by e-mail. Greg wanted to describe himself and his home to his friend. What kinds of measures and units would he use to describe:

1. How tall he was?
2. The width of his house?
3. How far it was to his school?
4. How much water there was in his swimming pool?
5. How much soda pop he drank in a day?
6. The distance he walked to school?
7. How fast he walked to school?
8. How fast his father drove on the highway?
9. How fast his computer was?
10. The size of his computer?
11. How heavy his backpack was?
12. How much vitamin C he took each day?
13. How big his father's truck was?
14. How much gold there was in his new class ring?
15. How long his school day was?
16. How long before they could see each other at Christmas vacation?

Some of these were more difficult to measure. But Greg used what he knew to find out what he did not know. What easy measures would help find the harder measures of 3, 6, 7, and 13? He also used some instruments. What instruments could you use to measure each of these?

Greg had another friend who lived in Canada. What kind of measures would he need to describe 2, 5, 6, and 11? Which measures would be the same?

We need consensus. If an inch is a unit of measure that we use to describe the length of an object, then we all have to agree on and know how long an inch is. If a paper clip is the unit of measure, then it has to be the same size clip all the time.

5. Most of our units of measure are standard units. Standard units or systems of units are decided upon by governments or, in primitive societies, by agreements between individuals.

6. Different governments have different measures.

7. Units of measures can be grouped into larger units. The size of the grouping also has to be by consensus. Larger units (groups of smaller ones) make it easier to measure larger sizes of properties. Smaller units and parts of units allow us to measure smaller properties and be more exact.

8. When communicating about measures, larger units can be exchanged (traded) for their smaller sized units based on the agreed upon or consensus equalities. The smaller ones can be grouped into the larger ones.

9. The equalities of the smaller and larger units are often designed to make exchanges easy. The best example of this is the metric system, which, like our number system, is a base 10 system. There are similar reasons for other groups of units. The size of a foot (about the size of a king's foot) actually was agreed on before the smaller inches. But it was decided that it would be useful to divide it into 12 inches because the number 12 has so many factors, and so fractions of the foot can be traded easily for inches.

10. When trading a number of smaller sized units for larger ones, there will always be a fewer number of larger ones. And when trading larger ones for smaller ones, there will be more of the smaller ones.

11. Measuring instruments help us make accurate measures, but it is always helpful to estimate first.

12. Measures help us make better models of the real thing.

Elena and Jose wanted to test their model cars to see which was the fastest. They built a ramp to test them with. What measures could they use to compare their cars?

Hint: There many be more than one measure that can be used. What units of these measures would they use? If these were real cars, would they use the same units? Explain your answer. What else besides the cars themselves would have an effect on these measures?

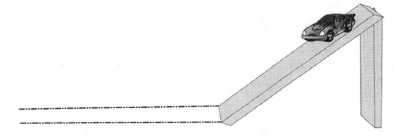

113 Students need to practice measuring with standard instruments that have the units already embedded and the nonstandard units they decide upon themselves in a collective consensus for sharing. The need for alignment of the instrument unit edge and the measured object is a critical beginning skill. The need to avoid any gaps is also important. Later, an analysis of the precision of the instrument should also be considered.

119 The transitions from straight-line measures to the concepts of perimeter and area require careful scaffolding and experience. The concept of perimeter as the total distance around the edge of an object or the sum of its individual sides is not difficult, but when the concept of area is introduced, the two measures are sometimes confused. Students should understand that the two measures tell about different properties but are nevertheless related. Connecting the two with problems such as the one opposite should help (see also #157).

Even adults sometimes have difficulty in expressing just what area is. Color tiles work very well in establishing the idea of square units as a measure of area (a particular space on a flat surface), but centimeter graph paper encourages the connections to actual metric units as well.

Brian and Ian measured their desks with blocks and with the same 12-inch ruler. Brian measured five blocks or 14 inches. Ian measured five blocks or 15 inches. What may have caused their measures with the blocks to be the same and the measures with the ruler different?

Mr. Torres wanted to plan out the new tool shed he was building so he made a sketch on graph paper in which each centimeter on the paper was equal to one meter. He wanted his shed to be six meters wide and 3 meters deep.

How can he measure how many meters of wall he will need for his shed? What do we call that measure? How many meters of wall will he need? He also wanted to find out how much room he would have for his tools. How can he measure this space? Can you see a unit of measure in his picture that would help him tell how large it is? What do we call this measure? How is it different from the measurement for walls? How many units of space will there be in the shed?

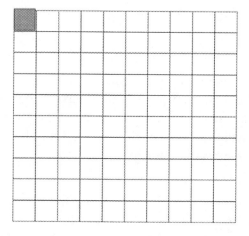

121 Teachers can help students develop the algorithm for finding the area of a right triangle by constructing a diagonal for a square or rectangle and measuring the area of the two to discover that the area is ½ the area of the rectangle or ½ (L × W). They can also reverse the procedure and construct a rectangle from two duplicate right triangles. This can also be done on the computer with a simple drawing program. (Note: Any two congruent triangles can be formed into a rectangle if one of them is cut through the altitude. Students can then see that the rectangle formed has the altitude as one side and the base of the triangle as the other. This develops the algorithm for the area of any triangle as ½ [B × H].)

122 There are several critical concepts in measures of mass
** and weight.
129

1. The measures of mass and weight are used interchangeably even though they have different meanings because our standards for mass are based on their weight on earth. However, although the mass of objects stays the same in space, the weight varies with gravity.

2. We measure mass by measuring the force of gravity on the mass. The force of gravity increases with mass. We can do this by balancing an unknown mass with the standard measure. When using a balance scale, we balance the unknown quantity with a known standard weight (one decided by governments or consensus) on a fulcrum. A good activity for students is to use loose sand in plastic bags and a spring scale to make their own standard equivalents for the pound, ounce, gram, and kilogram. These can then be used on a simple balance.

Chris wanted to find the area of a triangular piece of wood he was using to build a model plane. He traced the piece, which had a right angle, on paper and realized that if he turned the piece around he could make a square from his original tracing. Do you see a way for him to use the square to find out how large the area of the triangle is? How large is it if each side of the square is four inches? Explain how you found your answer. Prove the answer by making a diagram on centimeter grid paper.

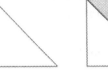

Cut two exact triangles from your centimeter paper that have a base that is eight centimeters and a side (altitude) that is five centimeters. Put them together to form a rectangle. What is the area of the rectangle? Compute the area of the triangle the way you did for the above, and then prove your answer by counting the squares on your paper.

Jerry wanted to weigh his big history book on a balance. He had made bags of sand to use as standards. He needed one 1-kilogram bag, one ½-kilogram bag, and seven 1-gram bags. How much did his book weigh? About how much did it weigh in English (customary) standard measures?

122 We can also measure mass by seeing how much force it
** exerts on a spring. The standard is actually in the resilience
129 of the spring. The greater the mass, the more the spring
gives. Many commonly used scales have springs inside of
them (demonstrate a simple spring scale).

Students should have opportunities to measure
mass/weight in both metric and English (customary)
units. They should also be able to estimate the feel of a
pound of weight as opposed to an ounce, a gram, or a
kilogram.

Measures in units of mass are good applications for
developing the general concepts listed above. For
example, it makes no sense to measure vitamin pills in
pounds or truckloads of gravel in ounces. Conversion
estimates that should be automatized include that the
kilogram is a little more than 2 lbs. The consequence of
this is, of course, that one's weight in kilograms is less
than half the number of pounds.

Chester wanted to know how much a clock weighed. He first measured a
block with a spring scale that measured pounds. Then he put the clock and
the block on a balance scale. How much does the clock weigh? Explain how
you found the answer. Explain how the two instruments to measure mass and
weight work. Would the clock weigh the same on the moon? Would the
mass of the clock and the block be the same on the moon?

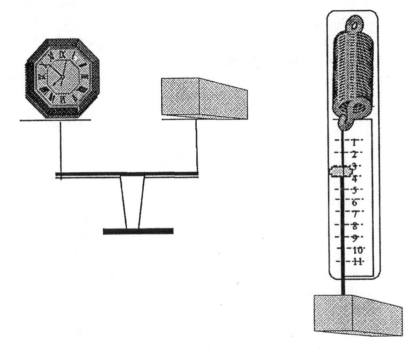

130 Although capacity and volume are related, they use dif-
** ferent measures. Volume is applied to solid objects that
135 have firm and measurable dimensions. Capacity is applied
to liquids and small grains that assume the shape of their
containers. It follows, therefore, that we measure capacity
by filling a standard measure (and not with a ruler). The
relationship between metric capacity and volume is that
one milliliter of liquid would fit into a container that has
volume of one cubic centimeter. There is no such rational
relationship between capacity and volume for the English
(customary) standards. There is even a difference between
the dry measuring cup for small grained flour and the
liquid cup.

Students often have difficulty distinguishing between the
two measures and describe volume with the capacity
definition as "how much something can hold." That, of
course, is not an irrational idea, but a solid object that has
volume may not have the capacity to hold anything at all.
Volume should be defined, in relationship to area, as the
amount of space an object occupies in three dimensions
rather than just on a surface.

Three-dimensional centimeter cubes are excellent manipulatives to help students develop volume concepts. Construction of structures, such as the one opposite, where
the area that an object occupies on the surface is constant
but the volume changes with the depth of the object, will
help develop clarity.

Sometimes, students will attempt to measure liquids with
a ruler. Practice with pouring liquids into different shapes
of containers and comparing them will reinforce the
concept of conservation and prepare students for the
measurement criterion of a standard-sized container for

measuring capacity. There are some fun puzzles involving
using containers to measure specific amounts of liquid
that students enjoy.

Choose a unit of measure for each of the following and
explain your choice:

1. The amount of rainfall in one day
2. The size of the head of a pin
3. The weight of a large truck filled with garbage
4. The amount of water a plastic soda pop cover can hold
5. The amount of water in the pop bottle
6. The amount of sugar in a candy bar
7. The total weight of a candy bar

Equal sized blocks were placed on a piece of graph paper that was
measured into equal rectangles. Which arrangements of blocks occupy the
same area? Which arrangements have the same volume? If each block has a
volume of 90 cubic centimeters, what is the volume of the blocks in
arrangement A? If the area occupied by each rectangle is 15 square
centimeters, what is the area occupied in arrangement C? Which
arrangement has the same volume as C, but in a smaller area? If each 90-cc.
block covers one rectangle, of which the area is 15 cm., can you estimate
how tall the block is?

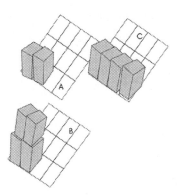

137
**
141
The measures of money, especially because of their relationship to our number system, usually do not present a problem for students—except for the process of making change. Their difficulty with change is probably caused by a lack of real experience, because today's cash registers automatically calculate change. Before this was the case, store clerks would count up the difference between the value of the purchase and the offered unit of money. The solution for our students is to provide simulated experiences of purchases. Class stores or computer software, even a free program on the Web, provide such opportunities.

A strategy I have used is to approach the challenge of giving change as "getting a fair trade." The item is traded for a unit of money that may be of greater value. The change maker must find the difference between the money offered and the value of the item.

To find the difference, we can subtract the value of the item from the money offered. However, in the action of giving change, we can count up from the smallest unit value of the item to the next largest money units until we reach the value of the money offered. We begin with pennies to the fives and use a nickel to get to the tens, or we may get to them without a nickel. Dimes take us to the dollars, but if we reach a multiple of 25, we can use quarters.

Problem-solving activities with money support the concepts of decimals and should be an introduction to, a major application of, and a reinforcement for decimal operations (see #100-111).

Mr. Berry's class ran the school store. His students had to give change when the purchasers did not have the exact amount. For each purchase described below, tell how you might make up the difference between the cost of the items and the money offered in exchange for them so that there would be an even trade. There may be more than one right answer, but try to find the solution that uses the fewest number of coins.

Money Offered in Exchange =	Cost +	Pennies +	Nickels +	Dimes +	Quarters +	Dollars
$1.00	$0.67					
$1.00	$0.53					
$5.00	$1.21					
$5.00	$3.28					

142 Beginning concept development of the measure of time should focus on the recognition of how different times of the day are related to different activities and events, on the instruments that measure time, and on increasing perceptivity about the relationship between units and time's passage.

How long did it take us to have lunch? To read that page? To play that game?

In spite of the fact that most clocks in common use today are digital, the rotary clock should be considered an important manipulative and visual for understanding our measures of time. It is also a reinforcer for fractional equivalents and, in some of its aspects, can be an introduction to the concepts of dealing with negative integers. However, as a consequence of the prevalence of digital clocks, the common usage of the terms "a quarter of" and "half-past" is diminishing, and the real-life vocabulary and experience that students used to bring to the study of the rotary clock are lessened considerably. Here are a "time measure" dozen concepts for students to construct.

1. We associate different times of the day with different activities and different events. Measures of time help us keep track of these activities and events and describe how long they take.

2. Clocks help us keep a record of the passing of time.

3. The actual length of a day and the number of days in a year are based on natural phenomena. The time it takes for the earth to rotate on its axis, or the time it takes for the sun to return to the same place in the sky, is 1 day. The time it takes for the earth to revolve around the sun is 365¼ days or 1 year.

For each of the three digital clock times, draw handle pointers that show the corresponding time on the rotary clock. Which clock tells the time that is closest to the beginning of the school day? Which shows the time that is closest to your dinner time? Which is the one that tells you when you should be in bed for the night? Decide which times are a.m. and which are p.m.

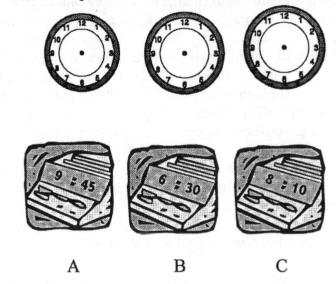

A   B   C

The class read a great story, had lunch, and then worked on their computers. They made a record of the time their clocks showed. How long did all three activities take? On the blank clock draw handles to show the time you think the clock would show after a snack break.

4. The division of the natural day into 24 hour parts and the hour into 60 minutes is a man-made standard. The natural day could be divided into other numbers of units that would be longer or shorter. The numbers 24 and 60 are useful because they are common multiples of many factors and therefore easily divided into parts.

5. Twelve noon is the time that the sun is most directly overhead or halfway between the east and west horizons. At twelve noon, the sun crosses an imaginary line in the sky halfway between the horizons called the meridian.

6. The 24 hours are divided at noon into 12 hours each of a.m. time and p.m. time. The beginning of the first 12 hours of any day starts 12 hours before noon at midnight, so we begin to count the 24-hour day as a new one at every midnight. Students will have to make a transition from their natural perception of when *their* day begins to the standard.

7. A 12-hour rotary clock can show only ½ of the day. It shows all of the a.m. hours and then the p.m. hours. Some clocks can show all 24 hours.

8. Because most of us use the 12-hour clock, we have to remember, when we try to count the time that has passed, that the clock starts over again at 12. From 10:00 a.m. to 2:00 p.m. is 4 hours.

9. Because the earth is rotating, the time of day is different at different places on the earth. When it is midnight at one point on earth, the place on the opposite side of that point or 180 degrees of longitude away is at noon. Therefore, we have divided the earth into time zones that begin in the middle of the Pacific

The earth rotates from east to west in the direction of the arrow in the map below. The map also shows some (but not all) of the different time zones. If it is 10:00 a.m. at point A, what time is it at point B? Can you find two places on a map of the United States in which there is a three-hour time difference?

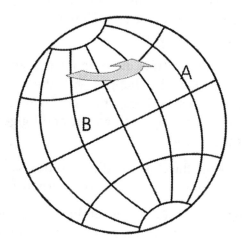

Ocean at the international date line. That line reaches the new day first and the rest of the earth follows. Just as there are 24 hours in the day, there are 24 time zones.

10. Because the earth rotates toward the east, we lose time when we travel to the east. The east is ahead of us. The west is behind us.

11. Because the earth is tilted on its axis, the number of hours of daylight changes with the seasons. In the northern hemisphere, the daylight hours grow shorter as we approach winter and longer as we approach summer.

12. We change the clocks at different times of the year to add more daylight hours to our normal wakeful time.

149 Beginning concepts for understanding the calendar should
** also focus on connecting it with life events and perceptions
153 of where we are in the present in the calendar terms. Naming of the days and months is a simple rote memory task, but understanding their sequence in terms of what day of the week it is today is more challenging. Keeping and recording a daily calendar helps, but kinesthetic games and visual enactments that clarify the meaning of "day before" and "day after," as well as the whole week sequence, will help the construction of concepts.

The connection between leap year and the fact that it takes a fraction more than 365 days for the earth to revolve around the sun is important. Memorization of the number of days in each month can be facilitated by a variety of mnemonics, but students should also know that these are man-made standards and that over time, there have been other calendars. There are even alternative calendars in use today.

Some students (and adults) have difficulty in predicting the date or day of the week for days in advance—especially when the date passes the end of the month. A problem often arises in the calculation of "If today (Thursday) is the 27th, what is next Tuesday's date?" This is a two- or three-step problem. Students have to count the number of days between Thursday and Tuesday and sometimes incorrectly include Thursday in their count. They then have to count the days until the end of the month and possibly add on the new month. Use number lines and enactments such as those recommended above to help, as well as real problems such as that in the figure below.

Starting on the 5th of September the soccer team had practice every five days. They also needed to play a season of eight games on Saturdays. The team wanted to know the days of the week and dates they would practice for 12 times and the dates of their games. We could use a one-year calendar for this problem, but it might not work for the next year. Explain why not. Use the table below to make a game and practice schedule for the team for two different years, one beginning with a Monday practice and another beginning with a Friday practice. Put checks next to the dates to note the practices and games.

Do you see any patterns that would help you make schedules in other years?

Yr. 1 Date	Yr. 1 Day	Practice ✔ Game ✔✔	Yr. 2 Date	Yr. 2 Day	Practice ✔ Game ✔✔
Sept 5	Monday		Sept 5	Friday	

154   Beginning measures of temperature should be related to
155   perceptions of how warm or cold it is. Activities can relate
a particular Fahrenheit temperature to whether or not a
jacket is needed—and whether or not it will snow. Room,
body, freezing, and boiling temperatures are significant
benchmarks with which to become familiar. Students
should also become aware of their own *normal* body temperature and how to read a thermometer. Normal then becomes a first look at the concept of range and average.
More advanced investigations of temperature ranges can
use original data retrieved over the Internet from all over
the world, and related to seasons and latitude.

Problems involving differences in temperature are useful
in reinforcing the subtraction operation. As skill
progresses, students should also be able to measure
centigrade (Celsius) temperature and be able to
distinguish the important benchmarks of each standard.
An important concept to extract from the much larger
range of degrees between freezing and boiling of
Fahrenheit temperature (32°-212°) is that each degree
Fahrenheit must be smaller than each degree Celsius
(where the range is only 100).

In reference to the thermometer, as an instrument,
students should understand that its use depends upon the
characteristic of materials to expand with increasing
temperature and contract with decreasing temperature. It
is, actually, a measure of average kinetic energy.

The zero temperature benchmark is also a good
application of the need for negative numbers. Problems
with negative integers may be applied to temperature
readings (see #10, 10a, 10b).

Two equal sized balloons were filled up with the same amount of air. One
was placed in ice water and the other in hot water from the tap.
Which picture describes the balloon that was placed in ice water? Which
describes the balloon that was placed in hot tap water?

1. Put the approximate temperature of the ice water and the hot
water on the thermometer that shows it best.

2. Underneath the thermometer, write the letter of the balloon that was put into
water of that thermometer's temperature.

3. How are the thermometers and the balloons alike?

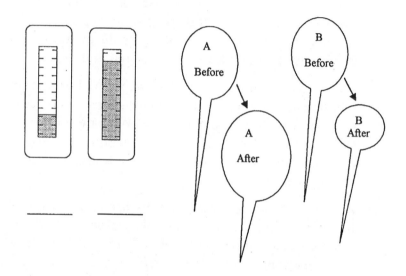

156 Beginning experiences with geometric concepts should fo-
** cus on helping students perceive and communicate about
159 the world around them from a spatial perspective. Seeing corners and sides or no corners, and describing what
you see, comes before counting and measuring them.

Manipulatives such as pattern blocks, attribute blocks,
and tangrams and geoboards can help students see the
differences and the patterns. Just the experience of making different patterns is helpful, but teachers need to scaffold the important concepts that can be derived from
them. In a triad, the manipulatives should be connected to
real objects in the environment and to the pictures on paper as both two- and three-dimensional representations.

What do we know about the shape of the Pentagon
building in Washington? What is the shape of the skating
rink? Why does it have that shape? Why are some places
called "squares," such as Washington Square? Have you
ever seen an intersection that forms a triangular corner?
Make a picture of it.

For some students, it may even be necessary to scaffold
the connections between real objects and two-dimensional representations on paper, or they will not make the
necessary connections. *Here is a block and a picture of the
block. Can you make a picture of just the top of the block?*

To distinguish one form from the other, let students
discover the nature of the differences.

*Run your finger around the circle block. How is it different from
the square? Why can't you put the circles together without
spaces? Why do we usually use square tiles for floors? What
other kinds of figures can we use so that there are no spaces? Can
we use more than one kind together in a pattern? Why do
spheres roll?*

Can you find some different shapes in these buildings? Name all that you can find.

Match the shape with how it might look from above.

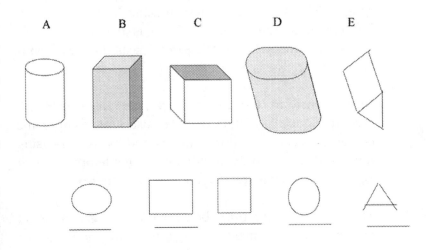

A   B   C   D   E

Why are some blocks hidden when we put them together? How can we tell how many are hidden?

If we join hands around the Halloween pumpkin and make a shape so that no one is closer than anyone else, what kind of shape is that? What does that tell you about the center of the circle and the outside edge of the circle? What do we call the outside edge of a circle? What property of the circle have we formed? What do we call it? How can we measure it? Make different-sized circles with a compass or on your geoboard. What happens as the circle gets larger?

To discover relationships between figures, students should try them out.

Trace two copies of your triangle (or use two tangrams) and cut them out. Can you put them together to make a square?

Make a triangle with one straight horizontal side and one straight vertical side on your geoboard. Make another the same size and next to it so that the third sides of both triangles are the same line. What figure have you formed?

Use wooden toothpicks or pipe cleaners to make a figure with eight sides. Without changing the space inside, divide each side into two so that you have one with 16 smaller sides. To what kind of figure did you get closer?

Let's draw a big circle around the room and join hands so that we cover the circle. If we change our shape to a square so that we can still just surround the circle we drew, can we do it with the same number of people? Where is the wasted space? Why are stadiums for large numbers of people in the shape of a circle? What do we call them?

Let students use their rulers and compasses or computer drawing programs to construct figures of squares with circles inscribed and circumscribed to discover the above

Mr. Taylor wanted to cover his workroom floor with tile. He wanted the tiles to be close together, without spaces in between. Which shapes of tile would work? Could he combine two of the shapes to make it work? Try some other shapes to see how they would fit together. What makes these shapes work? Can you find a rule to use?

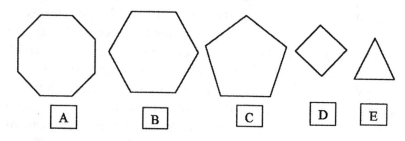

A   B   C   D   E

Can you find the hidden blocks in this picture? How many are there? How many would be hidden if we made this figure one block taller? How many would be hidden if we made it one block wider?

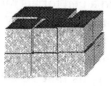

and other relationships between the square and the circle, such as the fact that the diameter of a circle inscribed in a square is equal to the side of the square.

To develop concepts that relate two-dimensional figures to their three-dimensional forms that occupy space, put two-dimensional construction paper figures of squares and rectangles together to construct hollow forms of three-dimensional figures, or pile up pieces of the almost two-dimensional paper to see how the forms are related. Trace an empty circular balloon and blow it up. Then, do this with the computer programs that extrude circles to form spheres, and create other three-dimensional extrusions. Connect the figures to the measurement of area as it is related to volume (as explored in #130-135).

Count the faces and count the corners of three-dimensional figures and compare them on a table with their two-dimensional counterparts.

Have students compare and enlarge figures constructed with pattern blocks. Use equally sized squares or color tiles to form various rectangles and discover the pattern of relationships between area and perimeter as the size of the figure increases.

A farmer wanted to build a pen for his rabbits. The cost of fencing was about $50 for a linear foot. What would be the least he could spend and still have a pen that had an area of at least 32 square feet? Use your color tiles to show some different kinds of pens that he could build. What shape would give him the most space for his money? How much would it cost him? Make a table record of the area and the perimeter. Look at the table and see if you can use your data to answer the questions opposite.

Robert built a larger figure using only his hexagon blocks. He compared the perimeter and area of one hexagon with his new figure. How many times larger was the area covered by the new figure? How many times larger was the perimeter? Explain why the answers are different.

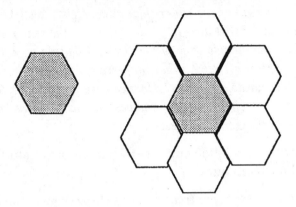

Why do builders like to build square houses?

What kind of a pen would you build for dogs?

160
**
163

Observations of symmetry in the environment can begin very early.

Make a picture of the leaf we found. If you draw a line down the middle of your picture, do both sides look almost the same? How are they different? Turn the toy car wheel or the plumber's nut around. Does it always look the same?

The observed concepts in symmetry can be strengthened by use of a reflective plastic Mira, which can support itself, or an ordinary mirror. The geoboard is also very effective.

Connect the terms that describe symmetry to common words in the student's language, such as bicycle and bilateral, radial and rays of the sun. Build the concepts with drawings and by using computer software that rotates and flips.

Try to name different transformations with the software or diagrams, including flips and slips. Use the term *congruent* to distinguish the fact that a transformed figure has the same dimensions and attributes, but it has a different position in space.

Would you be the same person if you stood on your head? Would you look different?

Use pattern blocks and other manipulatives to put figures together to form new ones, observing the effect of symmetry on the different possibilities.

164 Observations of symmetry patterns in number tables will help students automatize facts and strengthen number sense. Geometric relationships to number patterns, such as triangular and square patterns, are also useful in solving problems.

Jerry built two triangles on his geoboard and said that they were congruent. Alan said that they were different. Can you prove who is right? Build another triangle that is congruent to one of these.

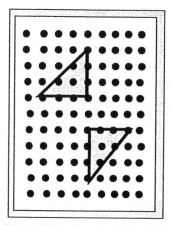

Use your geoboard or draw the figures on the picture. Can you put these triangles together to form a larger triangle? Can you form a square? Can you form a parallelogram?

If there is any symmetry in the way you put the figures together, show it with a string on your geoboard or with a line on the picture.

Certain numbers can form triangles and squares of individual objects. What do you notice about the number of objects in the rows and columns of square numbers?
If the number of rows is 7, how many columns would there be for a square number? What is that square number?

Square numbers: 1, 4, 9, 16, _____, _____
How can you tell if 225 is a square number?

Triangular numbers form different patterns.

 Triangular numbers: 1, 3, 6, 10, _____, _____

Can you find other triangular numbers besides those shown below? How would this help you in planning a brick wall for a pyramid-shaped structure?

165
**
169
The mathematical concept definitions of line and point can be constructed easily by students if they are given the opportunity to verbalize their observations.

How can you show me on your picture where your house and your neighbor's house are? How can you show me the straightest way to get there? The point is a location in space, and the line is what is formed when any two points are connected in a straight (the shortest) way. *Make five points on your paper with your crayon. How can you connect the points? What do we call the connections?*

The terms *horizontal* and *vertical* should be connected to objects in the environment. Horizon is the best for horizontal lines. An object hanging on a string works for vertical with younger children. The concept of *perpendicular* relates the two lines in an exact way, such as, "If you keep turning the two together so that one line is horizontal, the other will be vertical," or one of each kind meeting each other to form a right angle. In the beginning, relate the meaning of right angle to real examples from the environment: a building against the horizon, the corner of a book, a block on the table. Later, the definition can relate a right angle of 90° to the rotation of a ray halfway to a 180° straight angle or ¼ of a complete rotation.

One of the more difficult concepts for students in defining lines and planes is the distinction between a particular line segment or face of an object and the infinite line or plane of which each is a part. Students have to understand that the very particular language of mathematics is not the same as everyday common usage.

An example of the definition difference might be light, which goes on infinitely until stopped by something that absorbs it. If the light is traveling in one direction from the

Find the horizon on the picture of a skyline. _____

Find a horizontal line that follows the same direction. _____

Find a vertical line. _____

Find a place where a vertical line and horizontal line are perpendicular to each other. _____

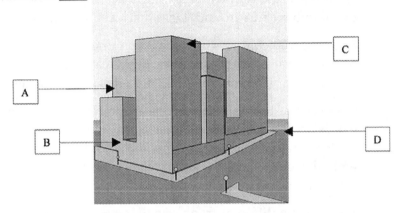

Jimmy thought about cutting his muffin through two different planes: ABC and DEF. What would the top of his sliced muffin look like if he cut through each of these planes? Decide between pictures 1 and 2.

Plane ABC _____

Plane DEF _____

Cut the muffin through another plane and draw what it would look like.

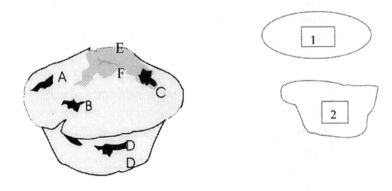

source, it defines a ray (more like a flashlight). If it is traveling in opposite directions (more like candlelight), it defines a line. The part of the ray or line from the light source to the place where it is absorbed is a line segment.

Any three points that are not on the same line form a plane. The top of a cube is part of a plane or a plane surface. An understanding of plane is important in understanding parallel lines, because lines are parallel if they are in the same plane, go in the same direction, and never meet each other. Lines in different planes could possibly never meet each other as long as they are in different planes but could meet if they were in the same plane. Lines in different planes often meet. Try cutting a muffin to show these relationships.

169 Beginning concepts of what is meant by an angle, as well
** as the comparative description of it as the size of opening
174 between two lines that meet at one point, can be related to real examples from the environment: the opening of a box lid, the mouth, the bend of an elbow. *Watch the stances of baseball batters. Compare the angles of their upper and lower arms.*

As described in Chapter 2, the exact measures of angles and circles should be related to each other. An important concept is the connection between the angle measure and the arc of a circle it describes—a full rotation of a ray through all of the angles describes a whole circle. Relate the man-made standard of measure of the full circle as 360 units or 360 degrees to the fact that the number 360 has many factors and can be divided evenly in many ways: $\frac{1}{2} = 180°$, $\frac{1}{3} = 120°$, $\frac{1}{4} = 90°$. If some confusion develops as students see the distance between the rays of the same angle grow, let them draw concentric circles or rotate another student at the end of a string to clarify the

Write the letters that describe:
1. A ray_____
2. A line_____
3. A line segment_____
4. Perpendicular lines_____

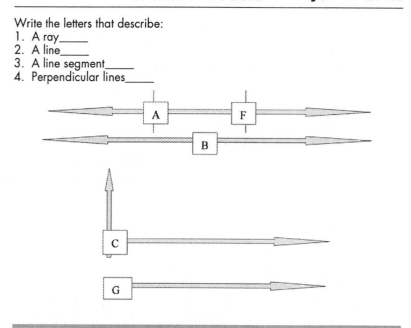

Find the angles in the batter's stance. List the angles A, B, C, and D in order of their size from smallest to largest. Can you find other angles? Show them and add them to the list in the correct order. Are there any that are close to a right angle? Do you see a straight angle? Do you see a triangle?

difference between the measure of the angle and the distance on the circumferences.

Discuss the characteristics of the circle in terms of its aesthetic and mechanical advantages. *Why is it better that the wheel doesn't have corners? Why do we like to see cylinder-shaped buildings? Why are targets in the form of circles? Why are flowers arranged in circle patterns?* Connect the circle to measures of its three-dimensional counterpart, the sphere, and its example, the earth, as well as to measures of latitude and longitude and the time zones.

Let students connect the construction of a circle with a compass to the fact that all of the points on the edge of the circle are the same distance from the center of the circle. The edge, which we call the circumference, is then the distance around the circle or its perimeter. Let students extend this through real measures to the concept that any line that goes from edge to edge through the center (the diameter of the circle) will be of equal length.

The Greek letter π (pi) may be the students' first encounter with a mathematical constant. Develop the meaning of constant from easier examples, such as four wheels for every car and two wheels for every bicycle. Then help them construct, by observation, the prediction that there is some *constant* relationship between the diameter and circumference of a circle.

Allow students to discover the constant themselves by cutting out and measuring the circumference and diameters of different circles, and comparing the measures in a table. Inscribe a circle in a square, and let them see that the diameter of the circle is equal to the side of the square. Thus, if the perimeter of the square is four times a side, the circumference of the circle just inside it is going to be just a little less than four times a side (the diameter of the circle).

All of the circles in the figure below are intersected by the same angle. For each of the circles, if the measure of the angle is 45 degrees, how many degrees of the circle is described by the angle? What fractional part of every circle is that? If the number of degrees in all the circles are the same, what makes them different? Before you could tell how much of a circle's circumference an angle marked off, what would you have to know? If the total circumference of circle A is 24 inches, how large is the part of the circle's circumference that the angle marks off? If the part of the circumference of circle B that is marked off by the angle is 2 inches, what is the circumference of circle B?

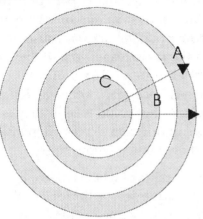

The diagram below shows a circle inscribed inside a square. What do you observe about the diameter of the circle and the side of the square? If the perimeter of the square is equal to four times the length of each side, what is your best prediction about the perimeter (circumference) of the circle inside?

A. It is more than four times as large as the diameter (or side of the square).
B. It is two times as large as the diameter.
C. It is about three times as large as the diameter.

Cut out at least four different sized oak tag paper circles and measure the circumference of each (with a string and ruler), and then measure the diameter. Make a table and compare the diameter and circumference for each. What did you discover? How close was your prediction? What do we call the constant that describes the number of times the circumference of a circle is greater than the diameter of the circle?

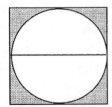

175 The most effective way to help students develop concepts and measurement skills for finding surface area is by providing discovery experiences that allow them to transform three-dimensional figures into the two-dimensional figures they know.

For example, they can discover that because there are six faces on a cube, the surface area of the cube is going to be 6 times the area of one face. See opposite for finding the surface area of a cylinder.

Janet wanted to know the surface area of a cylinder box she was going to decorate. She took a sample box and cut it out so that it was flattened into a two-dimensional form. She had the top and bottom and then a flat piece that was the length of the height of the cylinder and the width of its circumference. How could she find the surface area of the cylinder? What would it be if the height of the cylinder was 20 inches and the diameter 3 inches?

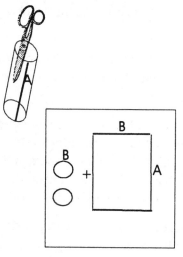

176
**
180 Data are the collection of measures that describe the world in quantitative terms. The value of data is in their ability to help us understand variations in our measures and the effects of measurable phenomena on our lives, as well as in their function as a basis for decision making.

The ability to collect and organize data is a critical skill in our technological and information-rich society. Students are constantly surrounded with all kinds of data that may or may not have meaning for them: baseball statistics, tickets sold to a new movie, weather data, candy and soda sales, political polls, crime rates, and population statistics. The Internet is a source of much real data that can be retrieved and analyzed.

The usefulness of data is determined by several factors that students need to understand, which they can—even at an early age—if attention is called to it.

The students in Mrs. Murray's second-grade class collected Pokémon cards. They decided to find out what kinds of cards were the most rare. They realized that they would have to organize their data and group it together. They each counted their cards and entered them on the following table:

Type 1	21
Type 2	7
Type 3	15
Type 4	36
Type 5	2
Type 6	23
Type 7	38
Type 8	9
Type 9	11
Type 10	24

Which card was the most rare and which card was the most common? How did the data affect their trades?

181
**
185
There are a number of overarching concepts that bridge the construction of knowledge about the different forms of representation of data. Teachers need to address these within the context of exploring the forms.

1. Data are only as good as the accuracy of how they are recorded.

2. The accuracy of the record is dependent upon the skill and honesty of the recorder and the instrument used to measure it.

   Provide students with shared experiences for recording data, such as taking the temperature of ice water as it warms and noting the differences in the records. Identify the variables, such as different students, different times, different thermometers, or different places in the room.

3. The interpretation of data depends on their ability to show patterns clearly. Proper organization and representation helps.

   Provide students with data-recording experiences that accumulate data over time and group data to show the patterns. Compare representations of grouped data where the interval is large to representations where the interval is smaller. If most people go to bed between 9 p.m. and 10 p.m., then a graph that has hourly intervals and does not show the parts of the hour between 9 p.m. and 10 p.m. doesn't tell us much. For the same reason, yearly rainfall amounts are elements that are best shown on a line graph in decimal intervals.

4. The kind of organization and representation of data that works best depends upon the nature of the elements of the data and the information that the data need to provide.

Mr. Edward's class was often disturbed by the loud noise of overhead planes, and so for a week, the students made a daily record of the planes they heard. They made a list each day and then made a graph to show the number of planes for each day.

Monday	✈✈✈✈✈✈✈✈
Tuesday	✈✈✈✈
Wednesday	✈✈✈✈✈✈
Thursday	✈✈✈✈
Friday	✈✈✈✈✈✈✈✈✈✈✈

✈ = One plane

What could they learn from their graph about when the noise happened?
What could have affected the correctness of their data?
How can they use the data to predict when to expect noise?
How could they find out if the pattern is always the same?
Do you have any ideas about what created the pattern?

Twenty students in Ally's class made a data list of their favorite Halloween costume. They showed their results on a pie graph. Which costume was the favorite? How many students liked that costume best?

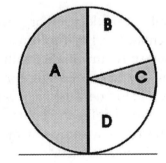

Legend:
A Ghosts
B Skeletons
C Witches
D Pirates

What two costumes tied for the second most liked? Which was the least favorite? From the pie graph, can you answer what the favorite costume is for the whole school? Explain your answer.

Provide students with experiences that demonstrate the different kinds of graphs. A bar graph shows the differences in the elements clearly but tells us less about the range and variations of individual results than would a line graph or leaf-and-stem graph. A line graph tells us more clearly where most of the measures are and where the exceptions are. A line graph also makes it easier to compare two sets of data, such as the amount of rain over a 6-month period that happened in the daytime compared to rain that happened at night.

A pie or circle graph shows little of the range, but it allows us to see the relationship of the part to the whole. For example, it is useful when we want to know not just how many students preferred the Yankees baseball team as compared to other teams, but also what part of the whole class the Yankees fans represent.

5. The interpretation of data must consider the many other variables that may affect it.

Provide students with poll-taking experiences to demonstrate that answers are sometimes affected by who asks the questions and how they are asked.

When making records of plant growth, point out the need to control all of the variables except the one you are measuring. If your measures are of the effect of light, then the water and temperature must be the same.

6. To make sense, graphic representations must have reference lines, or beginning points from which the differences in elements are measured. The reference line is usually a horizontal or vertical line on which the names of the elements or measured items are

Below is a data map similar to those that can be retrieved off of the Internet from the United States Weather Service web site (http://www.noaa.gov.html). What is the data element it displays? Can you think of a way to group this data that would help you see patterns? What other data might a farmer need to help him make planting decisions for the week of June 6? What other data might be useful in his planning for the year? Make one other kind of representation for this data. Retrieve a recent map from the Internet and do the same thing.

Soil Temperatures for the Week of June 6

found. Another line perpendicular to the reference line should show equally measured intervals from the reference line to allow for accurate reading of differences. Bar graphs sometimes do not have interval lines but show the measures on top of the bar. In a pie or circle graph, the whole circle is the reference, and the size of the arc that describes each part is the measure of the element. An arc of 36° is 1/10 of a whole circle, and so an element (e.g., kids with sport utility vehicles) represented by that arc would have a measure of 1/10 of the whole (number of kids surveyed).

Early experiences should focus on data to which students can relate, such as the number of brothers and sisters they have, the books they have read, the games they have, or the Pokémon™ cards they have. The simple pictograph is a good introduction to the graphic representation of data. Immediately, children can see the relationship between the item count and its representation on a line.

Later experiences should involve the collection of original data using instrumentation where appropriate and technology interfaces if possible. Students should learn how to make the necessary choices for representation and become increasingly critical in their analyses. The wide variety of representation choices in common spreadsheet programs makes evaluations of the appropriate forms a simple task. Ordinary graphing calculators now come with interactive temperature and other probes to take environmental measures. A vast amount of data can be acquired over the Internet. However, students should be able to evaluate data in reference to their own experiences with its collection and have the opportunity to use their own knowledge and creativity in its representation.

A three dimensional graph such as the one below can allow you to understand and analyze data. What does this graph tell you about the difference between the numbers of televisions in different communities?

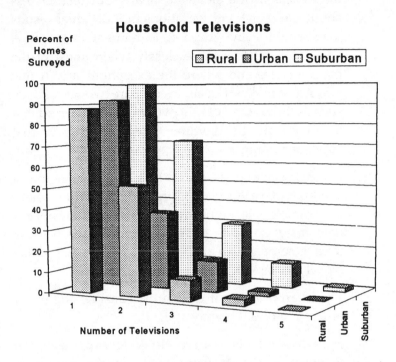

In what kind of community does almost every home included in the data have a television? Are there any homes that do not have any televisions? What could have affected the accuracy of this data? What could affect its ability to predict how many televisions there were in any particular farmhouse? About what percent of suburban homes had two televisions? About what percent of rural homes had three televisions?

186 Line graphs are useful representations that clearly show
** the distribution of elements. More than one line on the
188 same graph can compare distributions of similar elements,
such as the test grades of students in two different classes
or the variation in monthly rainfall in three different
places. Students should develop the following concepts:

1. The line graph has two reference lines.

2. The horizontal reference line, which can show different elements but often shows variations of an element
   over time, is called the x-axis.

3. The vertical reference line shows the measures in intervals and is called the y-axis.

4. The place where the reference lines meet is the origin.
   Parallel lines are drawn to both the x-axis and y-axis
   to separate the intervals and elements. The lines form
   a grid.

5. The value of each different element or the same element at a different time is a point on the grid. The
   points are joined to form a line.

6. We can also use horizontal and vertical reference lines
   and points on a grid to locate places on a map.

Provide students with the experience of making grid
maps of the school and locating places on it. Connect the
map grids to their understanding of longitude, latitude,
and time zones.

The line graph below represents the number of cars sold by a dealer for the first six months of a previous year. Label the x and y axis of the graph. What is the size of the interval? How could the dealer use this graph and table to compare the sales for this year and last year? Compare the table and graph to show the dealer what he wanted to know. What did the graph tell him? Can you write an equation that describes the relationship between the two years?

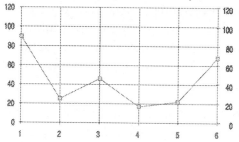

Month	# of Cars Sold in Previous Year	# of Cars Sold This Year
January	90	100
February		35
March		55
April		28
May		31
June		74

The camp director gave each camper a grid map to use in finding their way around the camp. There were three points that everyone had to know about immediately. Point A was the bunkhouse, Point B was the bathroom, and Point C was the dining hall. There was a spruce forest in between so the campers couldn't go in a straight line from one point to another. Each space interval on the grid was equal to 20 feet. About how far and in what directions did they have to walk from the bunkhouse to the dining hall, and from the dining hall to the bathroom? Add some other points to the map and describe where they are.

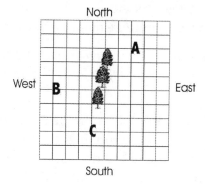

189   Studying a line graph helps us understand the relationships
**   and patterns in data and helps us translate the data into
190   equations or number sentences that show the relationships
as variables. For example, if we see that our germinated, fast-growing plant grows 2 cm every day, we can describe how much it will grow in any number of days, using symbols for the variables, as the equation G = 2 cm X D. The G stands for total growth, and D stands for the number of days.

Sometimes, we have to add constants. The future height and days are variables, but the present height is a constant. To determine the exact height that the plant will reach a certain number of days from now, we also have to add in the present height. If the present height is 4 cm, our equation for the height it will reach in any number of days is H = (2 cm X D) + 4 cm.

An extension of representations to negative quadrants will be a natural outcome of data collection that includes negative values. Allow students to discover the standard possibilities and invent some of their own. Connect to the study of integers (see #10a, 10b).

The concept of slope as it relates to the rate of change is explored productively by analyzing the representations of real data. Allow students to examine the various slopes of line graphs and compare them to the way the data change.

Look at the way the plant height changed. For every one unit of change in the day, how many units of change were there in the height?

Connect the word *slope* to the fact that by walking up a steep slope, you get up higher much faster than by walking up a gradual slope. Your altitude changes faster in relation to the distance you walk.

Ellen and her sister Sue were really good at making crafts. They decided to go into business. Each month they made a record of their profits in dollars and plotted it on a graph. During the fourth and fifth months they had to buy materials, and so there were no profits. From their graph, can you tell how much of a loss there was over the two months? Can you draw a line graph to show the same thing?

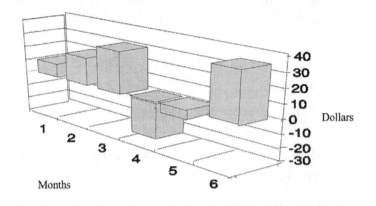

Randy's mother noticed that every time they added a new air conditioner, their electric bill increased quite a bit. New television sets didn't seem to cost as much. She decided to plot the cost of electricity against the number of each on a graph, which looked like the graph below. How do the lines compare? Which line do you think represents the air conditioners? Draw a line that you think might represent the addition of lamps. Draw a line that might represent what would happen if they kept eliminating television sets and the time they spent watching television. The angle that a line makes with the x-axis is called the slope. What makes slopes steeper or more gradual?

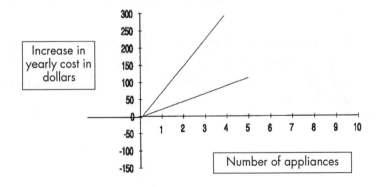

191 Beginning conceptual distinctions between the certainty
** and uncertainty of events can be developed as a result of
196 observations in the environment itself. Discussions of examples should include comparisons such as the following: the certainty that it will be day and then night versus the uncertainty that the day will be bright and clear; the certainty that it will rain sometime in a month versus the uncertainty that it will rain on a particular day. And transferring to other mathematical concepts, there is the certainty that if you walk in a circle, you will come back to where you started.

Additional developmental concepts include the following:

1. Being aware of and appropriately using language distinctions such as likely versus unlikely, and possible versus impossible, which are necessary for complete understanding. Clarity in meanings of the terminology of "event," "outcome," and "probability" are also important.

2. Knowing that uncertain outcomes and events can have different probabilities of happening. They can be more or less likely to happen.

3. Knowing that the likelihood (probability) of their occurrence depends upon the number of other possible choices.

4. Understanding that the probability of an event can be computed mathematically based on the number of choices, but realizing that it is still only a probability, not a certainty. There are only two choices for the toss of a coin, and so the probability that you will get heads is 1 time out of 2 tosses, but you can get 10 heads in a row.

The baseball team decided that they would use a spinner to decide what the positions on the batting lineup would be. The number spun is the position assigned. If a number already assigned is spun, the player spins again until landing on an open position. What is the probability of the first player who spins being the first in the lineup? If he doesn't get the first position, what is the probability of the the second player for being first in the lineup? Could the last of the players to spin be first up? How does th probability of being first change? When does it become zero?

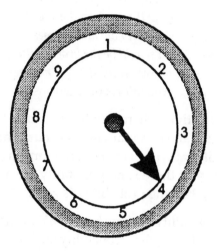

Spin your spinner 24 times and make a data table to show where your spinner ended. Combine your results with others in your group. What did you discover?

▶

5. Knowing that the more times you record an individual event or allow it to happen, the closer the data will be to the mathematically computed probability. If you toss a coin 1,000 times, the number of heads will be close to 500.

6. Knowing how to express the probability of an event as a fraction.

   If there are six choices on a die, then what is the chance for one of them to occur? What fraction describes one part out of six parts? (⅙). If you toss the die 360 times, and the probability is ⅙, about how many times will you toss a six? (60 times). What would be the probability of tossing a six if there were two sixes on the die and no five? Relate this to other ratio applications of fractions.

7. Knowing that if there is only one choice for the type of event and the necessary event occurs, then the probability of that type of event happening is ⅟₁ or 1 and is a certainty. If there is no possibility of something happening, then the probability is zero.

   The probability of a boy having a name is very close to 1, but what is the probability of his turning into a donkey? (Zero, except in fairy tales).

   Every other probability is therefore between 1 and zero and can be represented by a common fraction or decimal. The closer the value is to 1, the greater the probability that it will happen.

8. Knowing how to prove mathematical predictions of something happening (our inferences) by collecting data. *The more we collect, the closer we will be to our predictions.*

Three students tossed coins on a 36-square grid. Student A had 9 coins, student B had 6 coins, and student C had 15 coins. Who had the greatest chance of landing on a particular square? What was the probability for each toss? What was the probability of tossing "heads" on a particular square?

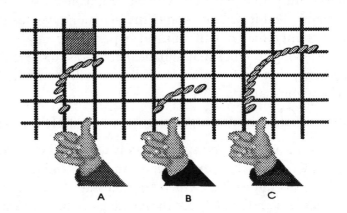

A   B   C

195 An understanding of the possibilities of different combi-
**   nations is necessary to predict their occurrence. The proba-
197 bilities of combinations of events can also be predicted, but we must first know the number of combinations that are possible. For example, the probability that today will be a Saturday is one out of seven, but the probability that we will have rain, snow, clouds, or sunshine on a Saturday depends upon the number of possible combinations and the probability of each. The possible combinations for Saturday with the four choices above are only four, but the possible choices for the week are four for each day, or 28. Computation of possible combinations in this case is then an application of Cartesian multiplication.

In the above example, there had to be a weather item for each day of the week; you couldn't have two days as a combination. In other examples where the items are interchangeable or order doesn't count, there may be fewer possible combinations.

It rained for 2 days in a week. What are the possible combinations of days of the week that were rainy days?

Because there are six other days for each of the seven, you might think that there should be 42 possibilities, but there are only half that number because the order does not count. Monday/Tuesday is the same combination as Tuesday/Monday. A tree diagram will show you the exact number.

Ball games where teams play each other are good examples to use. As long as home games are not counted as different from away games, the order does not count. Four teams can play each other once in six different games, but if each team has to play the other as a home team, the order counts, and it will be 12 different games.

The soccer league had four teams at different schools. If each team played one home game with each of the other teams, how many games would they play? If it didn't matter whether or not the game was a home game, how many games would they play if each team played each of the other teams only once? Why are there lines through some of the possibilities?

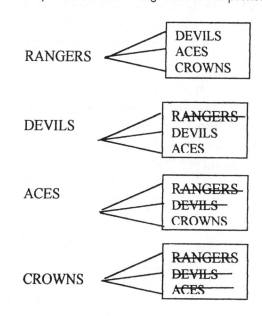

198
**
200
An important part of analyzing data sets is to look at how the data are distributed. Understanding distributions helps us make predictions and explain results. We are often interested in where the most events or outcomes are, but looking at the distributions also enables us to consider extremes or outliers less seriously. We also need to consider the range of possibilities.

Stem-and-leaf plots at the early levels can be used with single-variable data. They clearly show where particular values occur most of the time. Early vocabulary development includes the meaning of "the most," "around the middle," "typical," "range," and "average." Later, the terms *mean, median,* and *mode* can be related to these from the common vocabulary.

Computation of the average or mean should be put into the context of real problems. The Halloween candy problem is just one example. Let students have the manipulative experience of balancing the sizes of groups of objects as they develop the concept that what they have done is, in fact, divided, the whole being formed by all of the groups equally.

There is sometimes confusion with the additional terms *median* and *mode.* However, simply lining up the data in order and finding the middle of the sequence and the largest number of repeats is often enough to bring clarity. Drawing box-and-whisker plots should also help. Let students discover why outliers are less significant in computations of median and mode, and consider the kinds of decisions where these may be better choices.

The Girl Scout troop went trick-or-treating together. They wanted to find out what the average amount of candy collected by each Scout was. They put their candy on the table and, by moving the pieces around, separated it into

evenly balanced groups for each. When the piles were almost even, they counted eight pieces in most of the piles—although two piles were slightly larger. What was the average number of pieces a Scout collected? Can you think of another way they could have formed even groups and found the average? If the total number of pieces of candy was 98, how many Scouts collected candy? What could they do with pieces left over because there weren't enough to share evenly?

The students in Mrs. Boyle's eighth-grade class wanted to compare their heights with the heights of the students in Mr. Adams' class. They made a record of their heights and organized the data into this stem-and-leaf plot.

Mrs. Boyle's Class		Mr. Adams's Class	
Feet	Inches	Feet	Inches
4	7, 9, 9, 11	4	6, 10
5	0, 0, 1, 1, 2, 2, 2, 3, 3, 3, 3, 4, 4, 4, 4, 4, 6, 6, 7, 8, 10	5	0, 0, 0, 2, 2, 3, 3, 3, 4, 4, 4, 4, 5, 5, 5, 5, 5, 6, 6, 7, 7, 7, 8, 8, 9, 10
6	0, 1	6	

Can you determine just by looking at the data on the plot what the median and mode for each class are? What are they? How do the classes compare? What will you have to do before you can compute the mean for each class? What is the mean for each class?

How do the class means compare to their median and mode? Why did people think that Mrs. Boyle's students were taller? What does that tell you about the data?

What factors may affect the distribution of heights? How could they be much different in 12th grade?

Note

1. Pokémon™ is a trademark of the Nintendo Corporation. This computer game and its many spin-offs, including trading cards, are very much a part of the culture of youngsters. They can be excellent as motivators and as a real manipulative for constructing concepts.

Assessing the Content Standards

The Matching Rubric

The following represents a sample of how a matching general rubric and group or individual analysis of mastery levels might be used in conjunction with the individual items in Chapter 2 for assessment purposes. As suggested in Chapter 1, using the Chapter 2 master list of standards, teachers would choose the appropriate standards and decide on the expected mastery level for a particular grade or class. The concepts should be compiled on a separate list and shared among staff and parents, and perhaps with students. Alternatively, the feedback form can include a description of the individual concept, but this may make it too cumbersome. The assessment instrument would be matched to the selected concepts, and its substance is essentially described in the performance standard for each. For more detail on assessment and the use of rubrics, see Solomon (1998).

Explanation of Mastery Levels			
Level 1	Level 2	Level 3	Level 4[a]
Procedural exploration: Can solve problems based on this concept using the real or concrete representative materials, but is unable to explain concept	Concept mastery: Can solve problems and explain the concept used, but may still need concrete material	Procedural or alogrithmic mastery: Can generalize the concept and use it to solve problems without concrete material	Application mastery: Can generate an original problem using concept or apply it in an unusual way

a. This is an above-standard level that may be included. It is not delineated by grade level in Chapter 2.

Individual Student Feedback

Individual Assessment of Levels—Student Name		
Content/Performance Standard	Expected Level for Grade	Student's Level
17. (See standard list)	Level 1	Level 2
18. (See standard list)	Level 2	Level 4

Analysis of this report would indicate that this student is achieving above the expected level and does not require group or individual remediation.

Group Analysis

The following represents an analysis that can be used with a teacher-made test based on individual class or school expectations. The median expectations can be normed for an individual school population by comparison with previous grade-level tests, or they can be based on a standardized test that has been normed on a large population.

An analysis of the results below would include the following:

▷ For Concept 16 (rounding numbers one place), students in the class exceeded expectation.

▷ For Concept 17 (rounding numbers more than one place), even though the expectation was lower than that for 16, students did not meet it.

▷ This should be followed by careful analysis of the validity and reliability of item numbers 36, 37, 38, and 39.

▷ Individual and group score distributions should also be analyzed to make sure that a few outliers are not affecting the outcomes for a particular class.

▷ If the item is found to be appropriate, then teachers should analyze the materials and activities and revise them or plan additional ones for the group.

▷ Chapter 3 should be consulted for examples and scaffolds.

Class or Grade Assessment of Achievement									
Content/Performance Standard	Median Expected Class or Grade Achievement at Each Mastery Level (in percentage of class that reaches it)				Percentage of Class or Grade That Achieved Each Level				Item Number(s) on Assessment Instrument(s)
	1	2	3	4	1	2	3	4	
16. (See standard list in Chapter 2)	98	75	60	10	100	85	70	15	#34, 35, 36, 37
17. (See standard list in Chapter 2)	80	50	40	5	53	37	20	0	#36, 37, 38, 39

REFERENCES

Ashlock, R. (1990). *Error patterns in computation: A semi-programmed approach.* Columbus, OH: Merrill.

Baltimore Public Schools. (1952). *Arithmetic in the elementary schools.* Baltimore, MD: Author.

Baroody, A. J. (1987). *Children's mathematical thinking.* New York: Teachers College.

Battista, M. T., & Clements, D. H. (1996). Students' understanding of three dimensional rectangular array of cubes. *Journal for Research in Mathematics Education, 27,* 258-292.

Berlinghoff, W., & Washburn, R. (1990). *The mathematics of the elementary grades.* New York: Ardsley House.

Billstein, R., Libeskind, S., & Lott, J. W. (1993). *Mathematics for elementary teachers.* Reading, MA: Addison-Wesley.

Burns, M. (1987). *A collection of math lessons: From grades 3 through 6.* White Plains, NY: Math Solutions.

Burns, M., & Humphreys, C. (1990). *A collection of math lessons: From grades 6 through 8.* White Plains, NY: Math Solutions.

Carpenter, T. P. (1986). Conceptual knowledge as a foundation for procedural knowledge: Implications from research on the initial learning of arithmetic. In J. Hiebert (Ed.), *Conceptual and procedural knowledge: The case of mathematics* (pp. 113-132). Hillsdale, NJ: Lawrence Erlbaum.

Cathcart, G., & Kirkpatrick, J. (Eds.). (1979). *Organizing data and dealing with uncertainty.* Reston, VA: National Council of Teachers of Mathematics.

Cobb, P. (1990). Multiple perspectives. In L. P. Steffe & T. Wood (Eds.), *Transforming children's mathematics education: International perspectives* (pp. 200-215). Hillsdale, NJ: Lawrence Erlbaum.

Coburn, T. (1989). The role of computation in changing mathematics curriculum. In P. H. Trafton & A. P. Shulte (Eds.), *New directions for elementary mathematics: 1989 yearbook.* Reston, VA: National Council of Teachers of Mathematics.

Curcio, F. (Ed.). (1991). *Grades 5-8 addenda series*. Reston, VA: National Council of Teachers of Mathematics.

Fendel, D., Resek, D., Alper, L., & Fraser, S. (1996). *Baker's choice: A unit of high school mathematics* (Interactive mathematics program). Berkeley, CA: Key Curriculum Press.

Fennema, E., Carpenter, T., & Lamon, S. (1991). *Integrating research on teaching and learning mathematics*. Albany: State University of New York Press.

Fey, J. (1992). *Calculators in mathematics education*. Reston, VA: National Council of Teachers of Mathematics.

Fuson, K. C. (1990). Issues in place-value and multi-digit addition and subtraction learning and teaching. *Journal of Research in Mathematics Education, 21*, 273-280.

Fuson, K., & Briars, D. J. (1990). Using a base-ten blocks learning/teaching approach for first and second grade place value and multidigit addition and subtraction. *Journal for Research in Mathematics Education, 21*, 180-206.

Fuson, K., Wearne, D., Hiebert, J., Murray, H., Human, P., Olivier, A. L., Carpenter, T., & Fennema, E. (1998). Children's conceptual structures for multidigit numbers and methods of multi-digit addition and subtraction. *Journal for Research in Mathematics Education, 28*, 130-162.

Ginsburg, H. (Ed.). (1983). *The development of mathematical thinking*. New York: Academic Press.

Ginsburg, H. (1989). *Children's arithmetic: How they learn it and how you teach it*. Austin, TX: Pro-Ed.

Greenleaf, B. (1872). *New practical arithmetic*. Boston, MA: Robert Davis.

Grossnickle, F., Perry, L., & Reckzeh, J. (1990). *Discovering meanings in elementary school mathematics*. Fort Worth, TX: Holt, Rinehart & Winston.

Grouws, D. A., Cooney, T. J., & Jones, D. (1988). *Perspectives on research on effective mathematics teaching*. Reston, VA: National Council of Teachers of Mathematics.

Haitians, J., & Speer, W. (1997). *Today's mathematics: Part 2: Activities and instructional ideas* (9th ed.). Upper Saddle River, NJ: Prentice Hall.

Harel, G., & Confrey, J. (1994). *Multiplicative reasoning in the learning of mathematics*. New York: State University of New York Press.

Heddens, J., & Speer, W. (1997). *Today's mathematics: Part 1: Concepts and classroom methods*. Upper Saddle River, NJ: Prentice Hall.

Henderson, D. (1996). *Experiencing geometry on plane and sphere*. Upper Saddle River, NJ: Prentice Hall.

Hiebert, J., & Lefevre, P. (1986). Conceptual and procedural knowledge: An introductory analysis. In J. Hiebert (Ed.), *Conceptual and procedural knowledge: The case of mathematics* (pp. 21-23). Hillsdale, NJ: Lawrence Erlbaum.

Hiebert, J., & Wearne, D. (1986). Procedures over concepts: The acquisition of decimal numbers knowledge. In J. Hiebert (Ed.), *Conceptual and procedural knowledge: The case of mathematics* (pp. 199-224). Hillsdale, NJ: Lawrence Erlbaum.

Kellough, R. (1996). *Integrating mathematics and science: For kindergarten and primary children*. Englewood Cliffs, NJ: Prentice Hall.

Kreindler, L., & Zahm, B. (1992). *Source book: Lessons to illustrate the NCTM standards*. New York: The Learning Team.

Lamon, S. (1993). Ratio and proportion: Connecting content and children's thinking. *Journal for Research in Mathematics Education, 24*, 4-46.

Lamon, S. (1996). The development of unitizing: Its role in children's partitioning strategies. *Journal for Research in Mathematics Education, 27,* 170-193.

Leiva, M. A. (Ed.). (1991). *Grades K-6 addenda series.* Reston, VA: National Council of Teachers of Mathematics.

Lesh, R., & Lamon, S. (1992). *Assessment of authentic performance in school mathematics.* Washington, DC: AAAS.

Mathematical Sciences Education Board, National Research Council. (1993). *Measuring up: Prototypes for mathematics assessment.* Washington, DC: National Academy Press.

Morrow, L. (1998). Whither algorithms? Mathematics educators express their views. In L. Morrow & M. J. Kenney (Eds.), *The teaching and learning of algorithms in school mathematics: National Council of Teachers of Mathematics 1998 yearbook.* Reston, VA: National Council of Teachers of Mathematics.

Mokros, J., & Russell, S. J. (1995). Children's concepts of average and representativeness. *Journal for Research in Mathematics Education, 26,* 20-39.

National Council of Teachers of Mathematics, Commission on Standards for School Mathematics. (1989). *Curriculum and evaluation standards for school mathematics.* Reston, VA: National Council of Teachers of Mathematics.

National Council of Teachers of Mathematics, Commission on Standards for School Mathematics. (1991). *Professional standards for teaching mathematics.* Reston, VA: National Council of Teachers of Mathematics.

National Council of Teachers of Mathematics, Commission on Standards for School Mathematics. (1999). *Curriculum and evaluation standards for school mathematics* (Draft). Reston, VA: National Council of Teachers of Mathematics. Available: http://www.nctm.org/standards2000

National Council of Teachers of Mathematics, Commission on Standards for School Mathematics. (2000). *Principals and standards for school mathematics.* Reston, VA: National Council of Teachers of Mathematics.

Nesher, P. (1988). Multiplicative school word problems: Theoretical approaches and empirical findings. In J. Hiebert & M. Behr (Eds.), *Number concepts and operations in the middle grades* (pp. 19-40). Reston, VA: National Council of Teachers of Mathematics.

Piaget, J. (1926). *The language and thought of the child.* New York: Harcourt Brace.

Piaget, J. (1977). *The development of thought: Equilibration of cognitive structures.* New York: Viking.

Resnick, L. B. (1983). A developmental theory of number understanding. In H. Ginsburg (Ed.), *The development of mathematical thinking* (pp. 110-149). New York: Academic Press.

Resnick, L. B. (1989). *Education and learning.* Pittsburgh, PA: University of Pittsburgh Learning, Research and Development Center.

Reys, R., Suydam, M., & Lindquist, M. (1995). *Helping children learn mathematics.* Needham Heights, MA: Allyn & Bacon.

Riedesel, A., Schwartz, J., & Clements, D. (1996). *Teaching elementary school mathematics.* Needham Heights, MA: Allyn & Bacon.

Riley, M. S., Greeno, J. G., & Heller, J. I. (1983). The development of children's problem solving abilities in arithmetic. In H. Ginsburg (Ed.), *The development of mathematical thinking* (pp. 115-200). New York: Academic Press.

Ross, S. (1989). Parts, wholes, and place value: A developmental view. *Arithmetic Teacher, 36*(6), 47-51.

Schappelle, B. (1990). *A search for a curriculum to promote number sense.* San Diego, CA: Department of Mathematical Sciences.

Schifter, D., & Fosnot, C. (1993). *Reconstructing mathematics education: Stories of teachers meeting the challenge of reform.* New York: Teachers College Press.

Schmidt, W., McNight, C., & Raizen, S. (1996). *A splintered vision: An investigation of U.S. science and mathematics education, executive summary.* Lansing: Michigan State University, U.S. National Research Center for the Third International Mathematics and Science Study.

Schonfeld, A. H. (1986). On having and using geometric knowledge. In J. Hiebert (Ed.), *Conceptual and procedural knowledge: The case of mathematics* (pp. 225-264). Hillsdale, NJ: Lawrence Erlbaum.

Science Media Group. (1997). *Assessment in math and science: What's the point?* Burlington, VT: Smithsonian Institution Astrophysical Observatory.

Silver, E. (1986). Using conceptual and procedural knowledge. In J. Hiebert (Ed.), *Conceptual and procedural knowledge: The case of mathematics* (pp. 181-198). Hillsdale, NJ: Lawrence Erlbaum.

Solomon, P. G. (1998). *The curriculum bridge: From standards to actual classroom practice.* Thousand Oaks, CA: Corwin.

Souviney, R. (1994). *Learning to teach mathematics* (2nd ed.). New York: Macmillan.

Sovchik, R. (1996). *Teaching mathematics to children.* New York: HarperCollins.

Troutman, A., & Lichtenberg, B. (1991). *Mathematics, a good beginning: Strategies for teaching children.* Pacific Grove, CA: Brooks/Cole.

Van de Walle, J. (1998). *Elementary and middle school mathematics: Teaching developmentally.* New York: Addison-Wesley-Longman.

VanLehn, K. (1986). Arithmetic procedures are induced from examples. In J. Hiebert (Ed.), *Conceptual and procedural knowledge: The case of mathematics* (pp. 133-179). Hillsdale, NJ: Lawrence Erlbaum.

University of the State of New York. (1989a). *Suggestions for teaching mathematics using laboratory approaches: Grades 1-6: Operations.* Albany, NY: The State Education Department.

University of the State of New York. (1989b). *Teaching math with computers: K-8.* Albany, NY: The State Education Department.

University of the State of New York. (1990). *Suggestions for teaching mathematics using laboratory approaches: Grades 1-6: Probability.* Albany, NY: The State Education Department.

University of the State of New York. (1996). *Learning standards for science, mathematics, and technology.* Albany, NY: The State Education Department.

Usikin, Z. (1998). Paper and pencil algorithms in a calculator and computer age. In L. Morrow & M. J. Kenney (Eds.), *The teaching and learning of algorithms in school mathematics: NCTM 1998 Yearbook* (pp. 7-19). Reston, VA: National Council of Teachers of Mathematics.

Williams, W., Blythe, T., White, N., Li, J., Sternberg, R., & Gardner, H. (1996). *Practical intelligence for school.* New York: HarperCollins.

Wood, T., & Cobb, P. (1990). The contextual nature of teaching: Mathematics and reading instruction in one second grade classroom. *Elementary School Journal, 90,* 499-502.

INDEX